PRAISE FOR:
The CANVAS *of* TOMORROW

Bishop J. W. Macklin is a master visionary and transformational leader who has transcended his time and left an indelible mark on the city of Hayward, California, and the world. His life is the paintbrush that God used to paint on the canvas of tomorrow's hopes and dreams with his own blood, sweat, and tears. This book will bless your life and allow you to see the beautiful tapestry that God created using Jerry Wayne Macklin as His chosen tool!

—REVEREND DR. CHARLEY HAMES, JR., Senior Pastor, Beebe Memorial Cathedral CME, Oakland, California

The Canvas of Tomorrow takes us on an extraordinary journey into a community-in-transition during the era of the biblical personality Nehemiah and into a community-in-transition during the pastorate of Bishop Jerry Wayne Macklin. Bishop Macklin invites us into the life of a progressive pastor constructively engaged with Scripture and pastoring on one hand and street gangs, police officers, city officials, housing developers, and business leaders on the other. With insight, *The Canvas of Tomorrow* introduces us to urban ministry strategies and practical biblical principles employed by a congregation, Glad Tidings, that transformed an at-risk neighborhood into a thriving community. I highly recommend this book to pastors, government officials, and scholars interested in the vital roles that congregations can play in transforming communities.

—DR. DAVID D. DANIELS III, Henry Winters Luce Professor of World Christianity, McCormick Theological Seminary, Chicago, Illinois

There is much rhetoric about change in the faith community. God's call to the church is to be the principal change agent, but sadly enough, we hear so few good Samaritan stories that strengthen the church's resolve to be light in the darkness. This book illuminates the power of the Holy Spirit in people who are willing to sacrifice themselves to free others from bondage. Bishop Macklin originated the adage: "The need is the call." His accounts of the dramatic change that sprang through Glad Tidings International COGIC inspire the reader to paint a grand vision for a new level of trust in God. *The Canvas of Tomorrow* teems with invigorating biblical and modern-day examples of God's faithfulness to effect change in communities and individuals.

—JOSEPH JONES, PHD, President, Fresno Pacific University, Fresno, California

"Faith without works is dead." Bishop Jerry Macklin is a man of faith who continues to "work while it is light." In these dark days of division, fear, hatred, and hopelessness, he reminds us that God has placed a brush in our hand. The canvas of our future awaits bold strokes of hope, infused with prayer, encouraged by community, and inspired by the Holy Spirit. I have seen the evidence of his humble, unselfish leadership as it transformed the community of Hayward, California. He shared it with us, and he's shared God's miracles with all who would open these pages. May God add a blessing to the reading and hearing of His Word.

—GREGORY K. ALEX, MA, CDC, Founder and Executive Director,
Matt Talbot Center, Seattle, Washington

In *The Canvas of Tomorrow*, Bishop Jerry Macklin takes us on the transformational journey that happens in a city when one anointed servant of God dares to dream, confronts the issues of the hour, and believes in the power of God to make all things new. Bishop Macklin shows us practical ways each of us can partner with the Holy Spirit to bring renewal to our communities. You will find inspiration and information for your calling so that God can use you in more significant ways in the days ahead. This book will help you change our world.

—DR. WILLIAM M. WILSON, President,
Oral Roberts University, Tulsa, Oklahoma

An honest confession: fewer and fewer books and authors capture my attention, much less cause my pulse to race in anticipation of their content. However, when I received a pre-release version of Bishop Jerry Macklin's new book, *The Canvas of Tomorrow*, that is exactly what occurred. Why? First, the man. I have seen firsthand the results of his visionary labors. I have walked the streets he names. I have spoken with transformed lives touched by his compassion. I have witnessed this man's impact on a city. Second, the message. I serve pastors across faith and denominational lines. I hear their cries, listen to their laments, and pray over their burdens. This book speaks from a shepherd's heart to a shepherd's heart. Let your heart experience renewal again in the revelation of *The Canvas of Tomorrow*.

—DR. CHARLES G. SCOTT, Vice-President of External Affairs,
Oral Roberts University, Tulsa, Oklahoma

Bishop J. W. Macklin is not only a powerful preacher and prophetic voice, but he is also a visionary and leader who brings real solutions to some of the most complex issues facing urban communities: homelessness, health care access, economic development, education, gun violence, and prison re-entry. In the aftermath of the tragic church shooting at New Gethsemane COGIC, Bishop Macklin's leadership in Richmond, California, brought together pastors, elected officials, and members of law enforcement to reduce gun violence. Out of this effort, the organization Operation Richmond continued this vital work. *The Canvas of Tomorrow* will not only provide a divine strategy for change, but it will also provide a blueprint for a movement. Bishop Macklin reminds us that the Lord has given us a canvas and paintbrushes of faith. His is a critical and timely message for those churches, leaders, and individuals who desire meaningful change and real solutions.

—MS. SABRINA SAUNDERS, Founder and Executive Director,
The One Accord Project, Richmond, California

Successfully navigating the course of modern urban ministry can be difficult—indeed, some think practically impossible. However, in *The Canvas of Tomorrow*, the ministry journey of Bishop Jerry Wayne Macklin and the Glad Tidings International COGIC has given us hope. It is a model showing us how to meet head-on, with faith and courage, complex challenges and transform a community in despair. Bishop Macklin has for years served as an exemplar teacher and motivator. I have utilized his creative, organizational, and motivating skills to help further the work of Christ around the world. If you wish to see the power of the Holy Spirit at work in a modern-day context, read *The Canvas of Tomorrow*. It will help direct your ministry trajectory and inspire you to greater service for the Lord.

—BISHOP CHARLES EDWARD BLAKE, Church of God in Christ,
Presiding Bishop Emeritus, Senior Pastor, West Angeles Church of God in Christ

BISHOP J.W. MACKLIN

—

The CANVAS *of* TOMORROW

Nehemiah and the story of one church in a challenged neighborhood

AVAIL

Dedication

*This humble endeavor is dedicated to my loving family
who has journeyed with me throughout these years
in ministry: Vanessa, my dear wife, our two amazing
sons—Jerwayne and Aaron—our three incredible
daughters—Mataya, Mallori, and Jessica—and our
sons- and daughters-in-love. Without their steadfast
love and willingness to endure the constant challenges
we've faced, the positive lessons and experiences shared
within these pages would have been impossible. We are
grateful for the grace of God that has rested upon us.*

FOREWORD

Before I met him, I'd heard Jerry Macklin was a remarkable leader. As I got to know him, I realized the people who told me about him had sold him short! I'm not sure what adjectives to use, but I can say that I've met very few people who have such a blend of exemplary leadership traits. Let me describe some of them.

Jerry has a compelling vision. From the launch of his church decades ago, God gave him a picture of transforming the entire community, as well as individuals and families. This vision wasn't written and stuffed away in a filing cabinet (remember those?). It formed his unique strategy to buy and refurbish distressed properties around the church to provide safe, affordable housing for people who are members of his church . . . and for those who aren't.

He is the consummate activist, getting involved in the nitty gritty of community life, relating to the poor, addicts, single moms, and those who have been victims of racial injustice. But he hasn't stood against the authorities, who are often targets of activist rage. Not in the least. Instead, he has become partners with the police chiefs, patrolmen on the street, the city council, and other community organizers. He has developed a broad and powerful network of authorities and organizations to change the culture of his community.

Some leaders respond to injustice by becoming hardened, angry, and demanding, but Jerry's activism is filled with compassion. When he sees a need, his heart breaks, and at the same time, he launches into action to solve the problem, making sure the people grasp the love of God as he uses his network to solve seemingly intractable problems.

I've known leaders who have built big churches and businesses, and some of them have come to believe they're the source of their success. Jerry realizes everything that has happened around Glad Tidings Church is a gift from his Heavenly Father. This perspective makes him humble, tenacious, tenderhearted, and approachable . . . and he has a fantastic sense of humor!

In this book, you'll read about at least some of the marvelous things God has done—and continues to do—through Bishop Jerry Macklin and his church. The stories will inspire you, but don't miss the most important part: Jerry's heart.

Samuel R. Chand

Samuel R. Chand
A friend of Jerry Macklin

ACKNOWLEDGMENTS

From our earliest days of ministry, we knew God was stretching us, but to what degree we could have never imagined. Looking back, we realize now how people in our lives deposited into our future. I had a praying mother and a tenacious father who, from my earliest days, convinced me that more was possible. As the first African American family to move into a segregated neighborhood, we learned to turn every obstacle into a stepping-stone. Today, my brothers and sisters know that whatever heights we are blessed to reach, we will always stand on the shoulders of those who have gone before us. They've made our climb possible.

Pastor Albert C. Macklin, III, will always be remembered as the New Sweet Home Church pastor who cut his church building in half. He transported the church four miles away into a challenged neighborhood following a bold vision, remodeling and expanding the facilities as a transparent community transformation model. He walked the streets with people he served; he was a pastor with faith, fearlessly establishing numerous drug recovery homes and changing lives. I did not know at the time, but he was painting on the canvas of a new tomorrow for the city of East Palo Alto and surrounding communities. With the principles mom and dad deposited in us, my brothers and sisters, over the past four decades, have stood with me as a constant source of encouragement, often reminding me of the words our mom would repeat almost daily, "Go ahead. You can do it!"

Furthermore, I am grateful for the unprecedented leadership opportunities in our beloved Church of God in Christ denomination over the past 40 years that have allowed me to grow and develop. I will always be thankful for the friendship and mentorship of Pastor E. E. Savage and Dean Oliver Haney, who encouraged me to reach for relevance in preaching. Roy and Mae Winbush provided a clear example of dedication to ministry locally and nationally. At the same time, Bishop Charles E. Blake, Bishop G. E. Patterson, Bishop George McKinney, and Mother Mattie McGlothen, allowed me the privilege of witnessing ministry excellence up close. These gentle giants in ministry always sought to push me forward, seeing what I often could not see in myself. Their ministries were a clear and undeniable demonstration of what faith in God can do. Pastor Booker T. and Mother Theda Wells, Lady Vanessa's parents, were a constant source of inspiration, setting the bar high as the first African American pastor to erect a church facility from the ground up in the state of Oregon.

It was in Macedonia Church, from childhood, that I recall the sign that my uncle— Pastor B. B. Alexander—proudly displayed on the wall with the words from Nehemiah 4: "And all the wall was joined together to the half thereof, for the people had a mind to work." Little did I know that, week after week and year after year, those words were being burned into my spirit and would one day become the mantra to which I would march as I faced challenges I could not imagine.

For the past 16 years, it has been my honor to serve with my esteemed colleagues on the Presidium of the Church of God in Christ, Presiding Bishop C. E. Blake, Emeritus, and today Presiding Bishop J. Drew Sheard. I will always be deeply appreciative of their support and the continuing encouragement of friends and supporters as together we have endeavored to advance the kingdom agenda around the world.

Here at home, I cannot take for granted the willingness and courage of those select individuals in the city of Hayward who walked with us as we dared to challenge the status quo. City council members braved the storm of criticism to stand with a church that could not be silent. Officers risked their lives believing our neighborhood deserved more. And, officials labored behind the scenes to move our agenda of justice, fairness, and a new tomorrow forward. Years later, Professor Ray Bakkee and his Urban Leadership University would select the Glad Tidings Campus as one of the multiple urban ministry sites they would visit. Although not his first visit, on this particular week, the streets that surrounded our church were his lecture hall, with buildings, properties, and community ministry now dedicated to the glory of God. How honored we were that this renowned professor would bring his students from around the country to study a model for ministry that was unfinished and, at that time, unnamed. Indeed, his encouragement, contributions, and wise insight were invaluable.

Looking back, I know now, more than ever, the importance of prayer. Thousands undergird our efforts through continued prayer and encouragement. I will always be thankful. For more than 40 years, the men and women of Glad Tidings embraced a vision that challenged and encouraged them to join us in painting on the canvas of a new tomorrow. It would not be just a few. By the hundreds, this core of committed believers stood with their pastor and the first family to challenge the status quo and paint in vibrant, living color a new picture of what not only could be—but by faith in God, *must* be. Midnight prayer walks, door-to-door witnessing, and a continuing endeavor to serve people were the work of this daring congregation. Words alone cannot adequately describe the sacrifice and commitment of this bold congregation of believers. Our Community Development Corporation was often on the front lines, leading multiple projects toward community transformation. Their faithful and committed work, untiring labor, and commitment made possible the expansion of the Glad Tidings Campus.

Finally, as the sun would set on the long and sometimes lonely days, and as the dangerous nights closed in, it was to my home that I would come. Lady Vanessa, my partner in ministry and life, provided our family with a loving home and a reprieve from the crises of the day. I realized early on that the challenges I faced were not mine alone, as my wife and children endured them as well. Today, the respect and love I receive from my family is a cherished gift from my Heavenly Father. Thank you to all who have contributed to this faith journey.

CONTENTS

THE VIEW FROM THERE AND THE VIEW FROM HERE

There in Shushan Palace, Nehemiah's heart was arrested as he witnessed firsthand the pitiful and disheartening plight of the city of Jerusalem. In his beloved city, "The remnant was in great affliction, the wall was broken down, and the gates were burned with fire." After a night tour of the deplorable conditions of God's people, Nehemiah spoke with great passion to the few men that accompanied him. "Ye see the distress that we are in, how Jerusalem lieth waste, come let us build up the wall of Jerusalem, that we be no more a reproach."

In 2005, after many delays, I finally accepted an invitation to join the National Prison Fellowship Board with Chuck Colson in Lansdowne, Virginia. By 1969, Chuck Colson, a celebrated scholar, "had reached the high point of a dramatic climb to influence and prestige. As special counsel to President Nixon, he was one of the most powerful men in the country—until it all came crashing down." When Watergate splashed on the evening news, "Chuck [Colson] found himself at the center of the storm."[1] Accused as one of the "Watergate Seven," he would eventually plead guilty to his crimes and serve seven months in Maxwell Federal Prison. He would then go on to become the founder of the largest prison ministry in the United States.

How a man, who many people called Nixon's Dirty Trickster, and a pastor in South Hayward's challenged neighborhood became colleagues, ministry partners, and friends is another story altogether. After participating as a board member with

---

1 Alyson R. Quinn, "Watergate: The Glorious Defeat of Chuck Colson," Prison Fellowship, 9 Apr. 2020, www.prisonfellowship.org/2020/04/the-glorious-defeat-of-chuck-colson/.

Prison Fellowship for a few years, I also agreed to serve on the Executive Committee. I became even more involved in strategic planning and ministry to incarcerated men and women.

As Prison Fellowship Board visited multiple facilities, I was honored on numerous occasions to preach. In particular, there is one experience that I cannot forget. Like Nehemiah in the king's palace, listening to the deplorable report of Jerusalem from his brethren, I, too, was gripped by an experience. It was not that I had an experience as much as an experience had me.

We had traveled to the state of Missouri to visit the Jefferson City Correctional Center. En route to the prison, our van passed Lincoln University, a famous historically black university. I had heard much about this esteemed university and could hardly hold back my emotions. I was not expecting that after traveling only 8.3 miles farther, I would find myself standing in front of a federal prison. We entered, not knowing what to expect. In short order, I was preaching. I discovered men who were anxious to hear God's Word. The Spirit of the Lord was present, and before long, there was a connection from my heart to theirs. When I began to close the brief sermon, I heard voices shouting, "Don't quit, Pastor, don't quit. Don't stop. Don't leave!" Time seemed to pass so quickly, and I was allowed to continue beyond the allotted time.

This period of heartfelt ministry was undeniably a moment gripped by the power of the Holy Spirit. But, why this moment, why this time, why such a profound impact upon me? Then, the light shined, and I began to understand. The distance between the prison, with 1,600+ incarcerated men, and Lincoln University, with 3,000 + students, was only 8.3 miles. Today's incarceration cost in Missouri is $22,187 per inmate; the annual tuition per student at Lincoln University today is $7,900. Over years to come, incarcerated men could reside in prison, just 8.3 miles from Lincoln University; 8.3 miles from an 8 x 8 jail cell to a spacious lecture hall; 8.3 miles of separation between a professor and a correctional officer; 8.3 miles of separation, from a college library to lights out. What one decision could have changed the direction of any one of these men? What day were they arrested—not by a lecture or a book but by an undercover officer?

Upon exiting the prison, I was moved almost to the point of tears. Could the voice of one Christian witness have changed the future of one man after another? Could one man with an easel, canvas, and paintbrush allow men to see themselves in the light of God's tomorrow?

After all, what could men learn in an 8 x 8 prison cell that could compare to what they would have learned in a university classroom? Here, these imprisoned men could not be supportive husbands, caring fathers, or men standing strong as lights in their community. Yes, this 8.3 miles of separation shocked me to the core of my being.

I returned to Hayward with enthusiasm and faith; I could hardly wait to resume our work on the streets. I was convicted now more than ever. It was not God's will for anyone to perish, and it was not God's will for incarceration to be any person's future. Regardless of their current lifestyle, every man and woman on the street needed to know that God had a plan for their life, and God had a canvas called "Tomorrow" with their destiny painted in living color.

It's not hard to imagine the familiar story from Mark 8:22-25: After praying for a blind man who wanted his sight, Jesus asked him, "How do you see?" The blind man responded, "I see men like trees." Jesus called the man back, and He prayed again. Jesus asked again, "How do you see?" This time the blind man said, "I see men as men."

Now, today, in your city, how do you see men and women? How do you see children and youth?

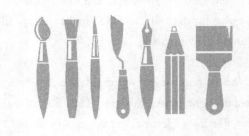

CHAPTER 1

WE ALL HAVE A CANVAS

Pick Up the Paintbrush

"Jerry, the word on the yard is that there's a hit out on a preacher in Hayward. Is that you?" The call came from Gerald Harris, my dear friend and former college roommate, who was serving as the associate warden in one of California's most dangerous prisons.

I responded, "Yes, brother. I'm afraid it is."

Few people thrive on change, many resist it, and a few feel so threatened that they'll do anything to stop it. As Glad Tidings shined the light of the gospel of grace in our community, lives had begun to change. Addicts turned from drugs to Christ and clean and sober lifestyles. Many marriages were performed, and more were restored. Dreams were birthed as men and women, young and old, picked up their brushes and began painting on their newfound canvases. A new sense of hope had risen in the neighborhood. This wave of love, forgiveness, and power meant that people involved in the underground economy and crime were given the opportunity to re-examine their habits, decisions, and futures. Like Nehemiah, I soon learned that not everyone was pleased someone had come to seek the welfare of South Hayward. The loss of revenue was more than upsetting to those who saw their income severely impacted.

At the time Gerald called me, one of my close relatives wasn't walking with the Lord. In fact, she had found herself in an exquisite home in Oakland Hills—the home of a major supplier of drugs to local neighborhoods. My wife, Vanessa, the kids, and I were sound asleep at 2:00 in the morning when the phone rang. I answered and heard a trembling voice: "Jerry, get out of there! They're going to kill you!" I asked for an explanation, and I heard this response: "I was in the room and overheard them. They don't know who I am. I was sitting right there when the man in charge put stacks of bills, thousands of dollars, on the table. He said, 'This money is for anybody willing to take out the preacher in Hayward. He's messed with our business, and now he has to go.'" Then she told me, "Jerry, you've got to get out of there. They plan to kill you!"

When I had hung up, Vanessa asked, "Who was that?"

I tried to minimize the threat: "Oh, you know it's going to be alright. Let's go back to sleep."

A couple of days later, the risk became more personal for Vanessa. She and our children were outside our home when a car stopped in front. The driver rolled down his window and said with a half-smile, half-sneer, "Mrs. Macklin, tell the reverend he sure has some cute kids." The car slowly drove away.

The next morning, Police Chief Craig Calhoun came by my office and soberly announced, "Pastor, we have good intel that there's a contract for a hit on you, and I don't think we can keep you alive unless we give you police protection."

Marked and unmarked police units were cruising all over the neighborhood. Hours later, police came to our home to escort our family to a safe location near San Jose. When we were moving in, I told Vanessa, "It might be best if you and the children go to Oregon and stay with your parents for a few days until the danger passes." I was very concerned for my family.

Without a moment's hesitation, Vanessa responded, "We're staying together—no matter what happens."

Later that week, we returned home, and the police gave me an unmarked car. I thought the danger had passed. I was wrong.

It was only a few days later that Gerald called to warn me that he'd learned some prisoners in a very rough prison in Salinas were talking about the contract to murder me. But giving me a verbal warning wasn't enough. He told me, "Hey, don't worry. We're coming up there." By that evening, several cars with dark windows were circling our campus. Gerald had recruited off-duty correctional officers to come to South Hayward. They were joined by uniformed and undercover officers from our local police department.

Word of the threat spread, and Bishop G. E. Patterson, our beloved presiding bishop in Memphis, Tennessee, called and asked, "Macklin, what's going on out there? Are you alright?" I explained the situation, and he prayed for my family and our church.

As I sat in my office, I wondered what steps to take next. I prayed, "Lord, You brought us here, and we're Your responsibility. We're going to live in faith!"

I began walking the streets at noon every day to show that faith is stronger than fear. The men of Glad Tidings often joined me, and then, to my surprise, some young men from the gangs came too. One of them spoke for the rest, "Hey, Pastor, we're going to walk with you. You need to know that we'd never mess with a preacher. It's not us."

The number of men who walked with me each day grew. I knew that a lot of men couldn't get off work to come, so I scheduled a Sunday evening walk around the neighborhood for 6:00. Our bold presence was to be a sign that this neighborhood belonged to God, but I had no idea who would be willing to join us in our dangerous act of faith.

On Sunday night at 6:00, I found myself standing on the corner of Tyrrell Avenue and Forselles Way at the front doors of our church. When I looked up the street, I saw a large army of men coming down Tyrrell. Many were well-tattooed, walking four or five abreast in the middle of the street. (I quickly realized this was either really good news or really bad news!) It was the pastor of Victory Outreach, a church that a few years earlier had been launched from Glad Tidings, and now had a large rehab home filled with men and ex-cons in recovery. When I asked the pastor where he was going, he responded simply, "My brother, we're coming to walk with you!" Needless to say, I was overwhelmed.

As the crowd of men swelled, someone tapped me on the shoulder and pointed behind us down Forselles Street. As I stood in total disbelief, my father and scores of African American men came from New Sweet Home, a church in what many referred to as "notorious East Palo Alto." My dad was rocking from side to side, pulling on his suspenders. As this large and determined army of men approached, I grinned and asked facetiously, "Dad, where are you going?"

He told me with a smile, "This is America, son. I can walk anywhere I want to walk!"

Hundreds of us lifted our voices and prayed. In the sanctuary, our sisters began to praise and worship which could be heard for blocks in every direction. We men began our walk around the neighborhood. People lined the streets like this was a parade. Actually, it was a parade—a parade of faith, courage, and defiance—unlike any other parade our city had ever seen. Everyone knew the backstory of the threats, and they wanted to see the outpouring of support from our community.

When we made our last turn heading back to the church, we passed the circle where drug dealers had operated freely for many years. By the time we got back, the street was filled with men, women, and children. Up from the crowd came a shout unlike anything we had ever heard before. All over the neighborhood, residents could hear the shout of the saints! Peace flooded my soul, and a sense of *shalom* fell on our community. To be sure, the fight wasn't over, but this was a moment that would always remind us that God's love and strength are more powerful than evil. I wish I could write more of this miraculous night, but even now, tears fill my eyes.

YOU, THE ARTIST

Each of us is an artist, and God has put a paintbrush in our hands. Talented artists "see" things others don't see, and their unique perception enables them to produce extraordinary works. This metaphor isn't blind idealism. The canvas on which we paint may be dark or light, clean or smudged, but it's the canvas God has given us to paint a masterpiece. We may have suffered (and may continue to suffer) abuse or abandonment; we may struggle with addictions, poverty, mental illness, or a pervasive sense of hopelessness. The message of God's grace and greatness, however, is that God wants to use every victory and defeat, every joy and heartache, for good—if we'll let Him. We have to see past the darkness and dirt to realize God's good intentions.

A young minister had a gift as a painter. Assigned to a church in a new city, he wanted to see his neighborhood close-up. He walked the streets where the homeless lived, and he saw a man in a watery gutter—passed out and lying awkwardly. The minister walked into a nearby abandoned building, went up the stairs to the second floor, and set up his mobile studio: easel, paints, brushes, palette, and canvas. He began painting. A couple of hours later, he came down to the street where the inebriated man in the gutter hadn't moved at all. He set up the easel and put the freshly painted canvas on it. He tenderly set the man up, and as he was regaining his senses, the minister told him, "I just painted your picture."

The poor man didn't know how to respond. "What are you talking about?"

The minister explained, "Here. Take a look. This is your picture."

Through his mental haze, the man stared at the painting, "That ain't me!"

"Oh, yes it is," the minister insisted. "That's you."

The man stared again at the painting. It showed a well-dressed businessman in a blue suit with shined shoes, a white shirt and tie, a nifty brimmed hat tilted to one side, a briefcase in hand, and a deliberate stride. The man in the picture was on the move to his next opportunity, full of confidence and energy. After a few minutes of careful examination, the man's blurred focus turned into a question: "So . . . that's me?"

"Yes, that's how I see you, and that's how God sees you."

The man responded, "Then what am I doing down here in the gutter?" He got up, dusted himself off, threw his head back, and walked off like a man on a mission!

This story perfectly captures my life's compelling theme:

If your circumstances are going to change, you must take the brush of faith and paint *in vibrant living color on the canvas of your tomorrow*.

It is the message and journey of my life, and it is the message of this book. It's a vision of a better future for every man, woman, and young person who would dare believe God: singles, couples, parents, employers, managers, and employees at every place on the economic spectrum. It's also a vision for pastors and church leaders who believe God can and will transform their communities. Go ahead, set your easel up, place a blank canvas in front of you, pick up your brush, and get ready to paint on the canvas God has given you.

IN THE HEART OF AN ARTIST

Whether an artist works with metal, clay, wood, paint, or computers, a creative vision is essential. Our lives, families, churches, and communities are the canvases on which we paint. Are we prepared? Will we seize the moment? As a husband, father, and pastor, I had to wrestle with conflicting desires in my heart. In tough times, there was always a crossroad—run *from* or run *toward* the fight. Would I believe God and be His trusted partner in the great enterprise of rescuing the world from sin and death? Would I allow God to stretch me, deepen my resolve, and sharpen my skills? Was I willing to rise above criticism, face the obstacles, and push past the fear? Would I complain, or would I seek the heart of God in prayer until I had His confidence and peace? I realized I didn't need a vision to do what I could already do; I needed a vision to do what I couldn't do. I desperately needed a vision to rise above mediocrity and timidity.

Let me ask you: What does your tomorrow look like? What canvas has God given you? How big is your vision? Is *good enough* good enough, or will you trust God for far more?

Beyond good enough, you'll find:

- » A vast terrain waiting to be conquered.
- » A breath-taking horizon waiting to capture your heart.
- » An ocean of opportunities of immeasurable proportions.
- » Resources you never knew existed.

To paraphrase King Solomon in Proverbs 29:18, "Where there is no vision, people are confused, disorderly, rebellious, and uncontrolled." But we need to be careful that our vision for the future is rooted in God's purposes, God's love and strength, and the values of God's kingdom. With Him, all things are possible. Without Him, we become self-absorbed, trying to fill our lives with things that look attractive but can't ultimately satisfy, like power, prestige, pleasure, and possessions. We become preoccupied with our preoccupations.

A WISH, A DREAM, AND A VISION

Far too often, we settle for something less than a compelling vision of the future. It's helpful to see the distinctions between a wish, a dream, and a vision. A *wish* costs nothing and often evaporates from our minds as quickly as it came. When I was growing up in East Texas, we couldn't conceive of smart televisions and streaming shows. Our entertainment was found in the pages of the Sears and Roebuck catalog. My cousins and I sat staring at the pictures, telling each other, "I wish I had that. . . . I wish I had that. . . . I wish I had that." An hour later, we were outside playing and totally oblivious to our previous wishes.

A *dream* involves us on an emotional level. Have you ever dreamed of someone chasing you or that you're falling off a cliff? How did you feel when you woke up just in time? Just before you were caught, just before you hit the ground? Sometimes the feelings are just as powerful as if the dream had actually happened. The emotion may have lasted for a few minutes or half a day, but before long, it was forgotten. You were back to business as usual. We can also daydream about winning large sums of money, being rich and famous, or having someone love us, but these thoughts also can vanish in an instant.

A *vision*, however, is bigger than a wish and more constant than a dream. In fact, we could say that if you have a consuming, empowering vision, it has you more than you have it! You know it's a vision because there's no price you won't pay to see it come to pass. You're willing to sacrifice to achieve it, and you won't stop until it's a reality. In fact, if you're not willing to pay the price, it's still just a wish, or at best, a dream. A vision isn't just what *could* be; a God vision is what *must* be. A vision is . . .

» A call to take action.

» A vivid mental picture of a preferred tomorrow.

» God's picture of the future.

» Your picture of the future.

» The ability to see something that isn't yet a reality.

» The assurance that God isn't finished with you yet.

» The determination to leave good enough to grasp something great.

» The reason to move beyond your comfort zone.

But let's face it. Even the clearest, most powerful vision can erode into mediocrity. When vision wanes, we need to ask:

» Did the demands of today crowd out our hopes for tomorrow?

» Did we become preoccupied with secondary things instead of primary ones?

» Did our vision hit the wall of unbelief?

» Did "the road most traveled" look more attractive?

» Did the necessity of waiting and working seem too high a hill to climb?

When the answer to any of these questions is "yes," we can keep wishing and keep dreaming, but the vision is in jeopardy. We can be sure it's a genuine vision—and not just a wish or a dream—when we're willing to pay any price to see it fulfilled.

A MAN OF VISION

Vision determines destiny. In this book, we're going to study the remarkable vision and leadership gifts of Nehemiah, the man God used to rebuild the walls of Jerusalem after years of neglect and ruin. I've often wondered if Nehemiah studied the life of Abraham. If he did, he must have noticed the difference in how Abraham and Lot saw their futures. The writer of Genesis described a moment when the two men chose the lands where they would live. Lot "chose for himself all the plain of Jordan" (Genesis 13:11), but this area included Sodom and Gomorrah, and "the men of Sodom were exceedingly wicked and sinful against the Lord" (v. 13). While it appeared the grass was well-watered, it turned out to be Astroturf. God told Abraham to go in a different direction:

"Lift your eyes now and look from the place where you are—northward, southward, eastward, and westward; for all the land which you see I give to you and your descendants forever. And I will make your descendants as the dust of the earth; so that if a man could number the dust of the earth, then your descendants also could be numbered. Arise, walk in the land through its length and its width, for I give it to you." —vv. 14-17

Centuries later, Nehemiah faced his own choice: to remain where life appeared to be comfortable or answer God's call to go where no one else was willing to go. Lot lived for himself; Abraham and Nehemiah lived for God's glory and pursued God's far bigger agenda.

When the size of a vision is comfortable, is it possible that it's too small? Does a God-given vision stretch people to pray more boldly and act more courageously, or must a vision be reduced to fit their current capabilities?

Nehemiah was a remarkable man who trusted God to do something remarkable. The people of God had been in exile for many years, and their homeland lay in ruins. The city of Jerusalem, the place where their temple had been built and the center of their faithful existence, had been devastated and plundered. However, God put it on Nehemiah's heart to go back and rebuild the walls, so the city could flourish once again. Was he qualified?

There is no indication that Nehemiah had a background in construction or engineering.

There is no indication he had an advanced degree in organizational management.

There is no indication that he had studied political science.

There is no indication that he had a military background.

However, Nehemiah acquired those skills exactly for when he needed to employ them.

We can't lead our families, churches, and communities to a place we're not willing to go, and we can't impart necessary skills to them if we haven't acquired them ourselves. It's not *who you are* that counts, but *who you're willing to become*. This is the pattern of the men and women in the Scriptures (and in church history) as they've been captured and catapulted by big visions.

Let's take a quick look at some people who responded in faith to the big visions God gave them.

ABRAHAM

Abraham left his home, not knowing where God would lead him. He lived in a country that was never really his own, believing in a promise that was slow to be fulfilled. Through it all, he became a man of great faith. In Paul's letter to the Romans, he described Abraham's trust in God through thick and thin: "He did not waver at the promise of God through unbelief, but was strengthened in faith, giving glory to God, and being fully convinced that what He had promised He was also able to perform. And therefore 'it was accounted to him for righteousness'" (Romans 4:20-22).

What would be different if Abraham hadn't been brave enough to answer God's strange call to leave home without a clear destination? How would history be different if he hadn't trusted God for twenty-five years to fulfill His promise of a child?

MOSES

For four long decades, it looked like Moses was a has-been's has-been. He grew up with power and prestige in Pharaoh's palace, but when he learned that he was an Israelite, he took matters into his own hands and killed an Egyptian who was supervising the slaves. Moses may have expected the slaves to rise up and follow him. When they didn't, he fled to the backside of Midian, where he languished for forty years. It looked like the end for him, but it was only the beginning. God called him to switch his focus from shepherding sheep to shepherding His people out of slavery and toward the Promised Land. There was probably no one more surprised than Moses himself that God tapped him for this job.

How would the story of God's people be changed if Moses had groveled in self-pity and hopelessness instead of responding to God at the burning bush? What would have happened to God's people if he hadn't pushed through the initial setbacks in his communication with Pharoah?

ESTHER

Esther had it all. As the queen, she had beauty, power, riches, and pleasure. When Mordecai told her about the plot to exterminate the Jews, she had to choose ease or risk death. To motivate her, Mordecai put her choice in stark terms: "For if you remain completely silent at this time, relief and deliverance will arise for the Jews from another place, but you and your father's house will perish. Yet who knows whether you have come to the kingdom for such a time as this?" (Esther 4:14). Through her courage, God's people were rescued.

What if Esther had told Mordecai, "No, that's not my problem. I'll stay here and eat bonbons." She could have sat on her throne and looked beautiful, but her people would have been slaughtered.

JESUS' DISCIPLES

I have a lot of compassion for the men who were Jesus' disciples. We can criticize them for being dense and failing to understand who Jesus was and why He had come, but we need to remember that they were following someone who was categorically different, in every way, from anyone they'd ever known.

When Peter and Andrew first met Jesus, they had been fishing all night but caught nothing. Jesus told them to lower their nets again, and they hauled in so many fish that their boat began to sink! At that moment, Jesus had brought them prosperity and a measure of prestige as outstanding fishermen, but when they got to land, they left it all to follow Him wherever He would lead them. They realized that Jesus was offering them something far better than wealth, fame, and pleasure. He offered them a life of freedom, joy, love, meaning, and spiritual power.

They were slow, though, to grasp the implications of what Jesus taught them. The disciples expected a messiah who would be a political and military leader to kick the Romans out of Palestine and restore David's kingdom. They had no idea the new kingdom would come out of suffering and sacrifice, humility and a cross, instead of the power of the sword. But after the resurrection and the coming of the Holy Spirit, these men "turned the world upside down." They may have been slow before, but when they got it, they were willing to do anything, go anywhere, and say anything to point people to Jesus.

What if the disciples had been so devastated by their failure to stand by Jesus when He was arrested that they completely bailed out on any future with God? They wouldn't have discovered "life on the other side" of their disappointment.

NEHEMIAH

Nehemiah had a trusted, honored position as the cupbearer to the most powerful leader in the world. When he heard about the plight of the people in Jerusalem, he could have stayed with the king and wished his people well. He didn't have to get involved. He didn't have to risk his reputation and his life. He didn't have to leave the familiar behind and launch out into the unknown. He didn't have to get deep in the weeds of a massive building project, laborers who had never built anything before, and adversaries who wanted him to fail. However, he answered the call and moved out.

The most important decisions are matters of the heart. When Nehemiah heard about the condition of the people in Jerusalem, his heart was broken. He had sympathy for them, but even more, he had empathy—he so identified with them and their struggles that he was moved to take action. He responded like Isaiah when God met him in His glory in the temple. Isaiah didn't view that moment as something God had given him for his own spiritual enlightenment; he replied, "Here am I. Send me." He was ready to go!

In an article written decades ago called "The Emotional Life of Our Lord," Dr. B. B. Warfield observed that the most common emotion in Jesus' life, as identified by the gospel writers, is compassion—more than all other emotions put together.[2] When He saw people in need, His heart broke, and He took action. When we're moved with empathy and compassion, we can tap into the heart of Jesus and become more emotionally alive. When this happens, we'll do whatever it takes to right the wrongs, meet the needs, and heal the hurts.

---

2 B. B. Warfield, *The Emotional Life of Our Lord*, www.monergism.com/thethreshold/articles/onsite/emotionallife.html.

Jesus didn't look out from the parapets of heaven at the depravity of humanity and wring His hands about *what is*, and He didn't stand back and give advice about *what should be*. He took on human flesh and did for us what we couldn't do for ourselves. He did what only He could do. He did *what must be done* if we're to be saved, freed, and empowered to follow Him to make a difference in this world.

God calls each of us to respond in empathy and action to the needs around us—under our roofs at home, in our churches, and in our communities. What are you painting on your canvas? Sometimes, it's as simple as mustering the courage to say those three little words, "I was wrong," followed by three more, "Please forgive me." Other times, we can take action to create new structures that have a lasting impact.

During the Clinton administration, there was a push to get people off welfare. I attended a welfare-to-work workshop to study the situation, and as I passed the Oakland welfare office, I saw a depressing sight. The office workers were separated from the applicants by a glass shield, anger and tension filled the air, and hope was nonexistent. The atmosphere in the room was depressing to say the least. I left that office confident that God was calling Glad Tidings to get involved and do something to remedy this tragic, debilitating situation.

After much prayer and many conversations, we began the Institute for Success to help people find and keep good-paying jobs. We lifted people's expectations and helped them develop confidence. Our main goal was imparting a vision, so they saw themselves with eyes of hope and courage. To everyone who came to us for assistance, we communicated a theme, a mantra God had birthed in my spirit, *Grasp a vision, make a decision, and move out! Someone sees you differently than you see yourself.* Nehemiah felt an intense burden, and his burden birthed a big vision.

Do you have a burden? Of course you do, but how are you responding to it? It's easy for us to minimize the problems we see ("It's not that bad."), excuse people ("He can't help it."), rationalize it away ("Here's why she acts like that."), or deny the problem even exists ("I don't know what you're talking about!"). To tackle a burden, we need two indispensable traits: hope and courage. We need a strong conviction that things can and must be better, even if we're unsure about how to take the first step. We also need courage to actually take that first step, and the next, and the next, even when we fall flat on our faces, we're criticized for being unrealistic, and people don't respond the way we had hoped they would. Even now as you read and hear in your heart the words from these pages, know that this journey is more than reading a book. It is a challenge for your future. Go ahead. Go as far as you can see, and you will see further. When you do all you can do, you will soon discover through the power of Christ that you can do more.

You and I have a canvas sitting on an easel in front of us, and God has given us a palette of paints and a handful of brushes. We can drop the brushes and kick the easel to one side, we can ignore them, or we can stick a brush in the paint and make a mark on the canvas. As we paint on our canvas of tomorrow, we need to pay close attention to the *Word of God* that's our source of truth, listen to the *Spirit of God* who is our source of strength, and spend time with faithful *people of God* who encourage us to keep going when times are tough. Through it all, we'll paint a new picture of our future—and it'll be beautiful!

A BIRD'S-EYE VIEW

A vision has two parts: the problem and a possible solution. The role of a parent, friend, manager, or pastor is sometimes to warn people that they're outside the boundaries of God's best for them. We don't delight in condemning people for their failures. Instead, we offer them a path forward and celebrate when they choose it.

I heard about three men who applied for a job at a major construction company to build a massive road with many bridges. The CEO interviewed the first man and asked about his qualifications. The man said, "I graduated from MIT with a degree in engineering, and I've written books on the kind of road and bridge construction you're going to do here."

The CEO then met with the second applicant. When asked about his qualifications, the man unrolled a list of freeways he'd constructed across the country. "I have experience," the man proudly reported. "A lot of experience. You can count on me."

Finally, the third man was called in for an interview. The CEO asked, "What are your academic credentials? Where did you go to school?"

He replied, "I've never gone to college."

The CEO was surprised, but he assumed the man had a wealth of practical experience. When he asked about it, the man shrugged, "No, I've never built a road in my life."

The CEO was puzzled. He sat back in his chair and asked, "So what conceivable role can you play in our massive road construction project?"

The man smiled, "I'm the guy who climbs to the top of the tree, looks out, and shouts to the people who are working below, 'Wrong direction!'"

Sometimes, our first big decision is to stop what we're doing, so we can change direction. The moment that Nehemiah heard the news about Jerusalem, that's what he did. He stopped what he was doing. He changed the direction of his life. And he served as a servant to change the direction of God's people.

That's my role as a husband, father, and leader. When I realize someone has slipped outside God's best, I step in to say, "You're going in the wrong direction!"

This isn't a rare occurrence. From time to time, all of us need to stop and change direction. It's called repentance, and it puts us in touch with the heart of God again— right where we need to be.

At the end of each chapter, you'll find some questions. Use them for personal reflection and to stimulate discussion with your spouse, small group, or other friends. This isn't a timed test, so don't rush through them. Ask God to give you wisdom and insight, and trust Him to give you all you need to paint a wonderful picture of your tomorrow.

CONSIDER THIS:

1) How would you compare and contrast a wish, a dream, and a vision? Give an example of each. What are the characteristics of a God-given vision for your own life?

   . . . for your family?

   . . . for your church?

   . . . for your community?

2) What are three factors that help people clarify their vision of the future?

3) What are three factors that can erode or crush a person's vision?

4) When God puts a burden on our hearts and gives us a vision to meet those needs, should we expect obstacles and delays? Why or why not?

5) What has God said to you in this chapter? What has God called you to paint on your canvas of tomorrow?

WORD ON THE STREET

GERALD HARRIS

Former Chief Deputy Warden, Salinas Valley State Prison

Those of us who have worked in the prison system have developed a sixth sense for picking up information, but it's seldom crystal clear. More often, we get bits and pieces of intelligence from recorded inmate calls and conversations, or a guard may overhear something and send it up the chain of command to our offices. When I was the chief deputy warden at Salinas Valley State Prison, I gathered information that alarmed me. A number of sources reported that a hit had been put out on a preacher in Hayward. My college roommate and dear friend Jerry Macklin had (and still has) a reputation for stirring the pot, and I was sure that if anyone had rubbed some people the wrong way, it was Jerry.

He had made some enemies in his community because God was using him and Glad Tidings to change the culture of the city. Crack houses were being cleared out and renovated for families, and drug dealers were having trouble selling their products on the streets. They were angry that he was disrupting and destroying their revenue stream—angry enough to kill. I called Jerry to ask if the intelligence I was hearing about a hit was about him, and he confirmed that it was.

I contacted people in our parole unit to ask for their assistance. They immediately went into action to secure Jerry and his family in a safe house in another city. Jerry isn't one to run from conflict, even a conflict that threatens his life, so before long he came back to Hayward. Vanessa insisted on joining him.

Instead of hiding in another town or in his office, Jerry made himself far more visible. He began walking around the neighborhood every day—in plain sight of the people who loved him and in plain sight of those who opposed him. Scores, maybe hundreds, of men joined him, including me. We wanted to show the neighborhood that his vision had become our vision, and his fight had become our fight. My sixth sense operates in every venue, and as we walked around the neighborhood, I could feel the tension in the air.

I was there because I love and respect Jerry, and I'd do anything for him. He was my roommate in college, and he asked me to stand up with him at his wedding. His children call me Uncle Gerald, and my kids call him Uncle Jerry. When we were in college, he often took me home with him to Palo Alto. His mother and father moved his younger brother Albert out of his bed, so I could have a comfortable place to sleep—and Albert got the floor. Jerry and I have been closely connected for most of our lives, and we'll always be close.

As a pastor and community leader, Jerry has always been lightyears ahead of others in his vision, courage, and ability to find necessary resources. When he sees a need, he views it as an opportunity to create change, and he's willing to tackle difficulties others shy away from. He's a genius in finding creative solutions to complex problems. At Glad Tidings, he started small and has trusted God to gradually transform the community. I'm proud to call him my friend.

CHAPTER 2

DO YOU HEAR WHAT I HEAR?

Nehemiah Heard What No One Else Heard

And we think we have it rough! God had done miraculous things to rescue His people from Egypt, give them strength to conquer the Promised Land, and build a kingdom unlike any the world had ever seen—following the One God of Israel instead of the many gods of the pagans. The freed slaves were God's chosen people, the apple of His eye, but they drifted away from God. Gradually, corrupt kings led the people in the wrong direction. God sent prophets to warn them and invite them to repent, but their hearts were hardened. Finally, God sent the two most powerful armies in the world, first the Assyrians and then the Babylonians, to capture Israel and then Judah, destroy the temple, devastate Jerusalem, and carry God's people off into exile.

The Babylonians incorporated conquered people into their culture. The history of Daniel and his three friends tells us that some of the Jews rose to high positions even as they were far from their native land. One of the Jews who rose to prominence was Nehemiah. He had been promoted to be King Artaxerxes's cupbearer, an honored position filled only by someone the king trusted with his life.

In the capital city of Shushan, visitors brought news to Nehemiah:

> *It came to pass in the month of Chislev, in the twentieth year, as I was in Shushan*
> *the citadel, that Hanani one of my brethren came with men from Judah; and I*
> *asked them concerning the Jews who had escaped, who had survived the captivity,*
> *and concerning Jerusalem. And they said to me, "The survivors who are left from*
> *the captivity in the province are there in great distress and reproach. The wall of*
> *Jerusalem is also broken down, and its gates are burned with fire." So it was, when*
> *I heard these words. —Nehemiah 1:1-4*

I can imagine that Nehemiah was fully occupied with his important role in the palace. His responsibility was to taste all the wine to be sure it hadn't been poisoned and to be sure it was the finest in the land. It's human nature: when we're preoccupied with what's right in front of us, we don't even think about what's going on elsewhere—until we hear exciting or disturbing news.

In this case, the news was alarming! Have you ever heard someone rush in the door and shout, "The house is on fire!" Instantly, you realize you have no time to lose. Your adrenaline kicks in, and you have incredible energy and clear focus about what you need to do to rescue your family from the flames.

The news Nehemiah heard wasn't quite like a fire drill, but it was just as dramatic. God's people, the ones who had returned to Jerusalem after many years in exile, were in deep trouble. Their defenses were in shambles, and they were the subject of scorn from their neighbors. Nehemiah probably had been singing the "songs of Zion" while he served the Persian king Artaxerxes (the Persians had defeated the Babylonians by this time), but until this moment, he didn't know that Zion was still a disaster area.

Would he ignore the news and go back to business as usual, or would he hear it as a call to arms?

Would he let the moment pass, or would he sense God pulling his heartstrings?

Did he hear only Hanani and the men with him with his physical ears, or would he hear the voice of God's people crying out to him for help with his heart?

Was God speaking to him through these men, or was it just last night's pizza talking?

HEARING GOD

When I talk about hearing God's voice, some people react like I've told them I've turned into a tomato. They simply can't comprehend the infinite, almighty God speaking to them. Oh, they believe God spoke to Moses and the prophets, and Jesus spoke to people when He walked among us, but today? Here? Now? You and me? They just shake their heads at the thought.

I want to assure you that God still speaks to us. John's Gospel tells us that Jesus is "the Word"—it is God's very nature to communicate with us. To be honest, I'm often more than a little skeptical when people tell me, "God told me this or that." I'm afraid that language is used too often to end a conversation. After all, who can argue with God? So, I'm sure there are some misunderstandings about the way God communicates and His purpose for speaking to us, but we can count on this truth which we find throughout the Scriptures and the history of those who believe: God is a speaking, communicating, engaged God who delights to connect with His beloved children.

But how does He communicate? In several ways. Perhaps most often through the Scriptures. Jesus is the Word, and the Bible is God's Word. Does that seem confusing? It's not if we realize that Jesus is "the way, the truth, and the life." When we read the Bible, we're reading God's personal letter to us. Do we see it that way? Most of us don't. If we read it at all, we read with a sense of detachment, more confused and distracted than engaged with the divine author. When we open the pages of the Bible, we can pray, "Lord, You're a speaking God. Speak to me through Your Word. I'm listening." There have been countless times when a passage "comes alive" with new depth of meaning and specific application to my life. It doesn't happen every time, but it happens enough to encourage me to expect God to speak through the Scriptures.

God often confirms the truths we read in the Bible by the whispers of the Holy Spirit. We don't have to invite the Spirit to come from far off—He has taken up residence in us. He has many roles, but one is to convince us that Jesus' payment for sin has accomplished three life-transforming things: We're totally forgiven. We've been imputed with Christ's righteousness. And we've been adopted as God's dear children. Paul explains the Holy Spirit's confirmation this way in his letter to the Romans:

For you did not receive the spirit of bondage again to fear, but you received the Spirit of adoption by whom we cry out, "Abba, Father." The Spirit Himself bears witness with our spirit that we are children of God, and if children, then heirs—heirs of God and joint-heirs with Christ, if indeed we suffer with Him, that we may also be glorified together. —Romans 8:15-17

The Spirit convicts us of sin but not to blast us with condemnation. He is our Advocate, our defense attorney who reminds the Judge of All (and us) that the penalty for our sin has already been paid in full, and at the same time, He reminds us of God's immeasurable love for us. Do you hear the Spirit speaking to you with this message of love and forgiveness? If not, it's not Him.

God speaks to us through other believers who are walking closely with Him. We need to be careful, though, that what we hear from those people lines up with the teaching of Scripture. Where they differ, we need to lean on the Bible instead of people, no matter how assertive and persuasive they may sound. One of the people God uses to speak to us is our pastor, preacher, or teacher, who shares the wealth of knowledge about God and His purposes for us.

I hear God in all those ways. The question is: am I listening? And a second is like it: are you listening?

How did Nehemiah hear God's voice? Through Hanani and his friends. Their message of heartache fit with what Nehemiah knew of God's will for His people—and he knew something had to be done to fix the problem!

CHANGE OF DIRECTION

In August 1978, with an overheated car, I found myself at the 76 gas station on the corner of A Street and Mission in Hayward, California. I was unfamiliar with the city. I was preparing for our first pastoral appointment in Louisiana, and I was running an errand. As I stood on the corner waiting for my car to be repaired, I heard a voice in my spirit, *Do not go to Louisiana. This will be your city.* I immediately rejected the voice. It seemed strange, even absurd. Hadn't we prayed and sought the Lord about our calling to the church in Louisiana? Of course we had. I wondered where this message originated, and I completely discounted it. A few minutes later, I heard the voice again,

Do not go to Louisiana. This will be your city. This time, I couldn't deny that it was the Lord. If this was my new calling, I wanted to see who might be coming to our church. As I stood on the corner, I didn't see a single person of color on that busy boulevard.

About an hour later, with my car patched up, I was headed back to East Palo Alto to share the news with Vanessa. I stopped briefly at New Sweet Home to speak to my father. I was in search of his sage advice. When I told him about the message I'd sensed as I waited for my car, he replied, "Son, follow the voice of the Lord." I drove a few blocks to inform Vanessa of my surprising experience over the last two hours.

Within an hour or two, we were on our way to Hayward. I'll never forget her invaluable support. Turning on Tennyson Road, the first exit coming into the city, brought me to a neighborhood I'd never seen before. Driving four blocks west on Tennyson Road, I noticed a small church on the left side of the busy street. I made a quick U-turn at Tyrrell, and we drove into the driveway of Evangelical Covenant Church of America.

My eyes lit up, and once again, I heard that same voice, *If you do as I have instructed, this will be your church.* I told Vanessa what I'd heard. As we turned to leave the driveway, the vision of the church was burned into my spirit.

A few short months later, Glad Tidings was birthed in our living room as a Bible study. Vanessa welcomed guests into our home each week and provided delicious meals for all who attended. Week by week, the Bible study group grew until we needed to find our first sanctuary. Eden United Church of Hayward was very gracious and opened their doors to allow us to rent their upstairs fellowship hall. We quickly named our new place of worship "the Upper Room."

Two years later, we at Glad Tidings held our first service in the church the Lord had first shown me on Tennyson Road. During those two years, I often drove by the facility on Tennyson and stopped next door at Winchell's Donuts to get a cup of coffee and a donut. For twenty to thirty minutes, I stared at the church from the parking lot. Although I'd never been inside, I gave God thanks for our new sanctuary. Like Nehemiah, I told no one what was in my heart.

On a Sunday morning, I entered through the side doors of the church on Tennyson to find a few people sitting in the fellowship hall. It was evident that most of the building wasn't in use. Later that week, I called the denomination's regional headquarters in Pasadena to inquire about their plans for the building and was directed to the general superintendent, Rev. La Vern Sands. He told me it was strange that I called because they had just been discussing their plans for the building. He asked how soon I could come to Pasadena. I answered, "Immediately!" Within a few days, I was on a plane to visit the regional headquarters in Pasadena.

It wasn't long before I responded to the Evangelical Covenant Church with a letter of intent to ask how we could acquire the facilities. The process took an entire year of back-and-forth negotiations. Within a few months, however, we found ourselves competing with several other churches who not only wanted the facility but were more financially able to acquire the church. Our original offer was $170,000, but we soon realized we would have to increase our offer—and we did—to $200,000. The problem was there were two or three other churches whose offers exceeded ours, and they were willing to pay cash. It didn't look good for us.

We had no cash, but we trusted God to provide. In the end, it came down to a final board meeting that was to be held on a conference call with members of the Evangelical Covenant Executive Board. Once we knew the date for this call, we prayed. The Lord led us to begin a signature petition in the neighborhood the weekend before the call to ask residents to sign in support of Glad Tidings coming to South Hayward. We collected hundreds of signatures in one weekend and made multiple copies, one for each board member. At the same time, a dear friend and professor shared a creative approach with me: We weren't acquiring the church based only on our ability to finance it but on the calling of the denomination to that neighborhood. We weren't asking to purchase the church; we were asking the denomination to allow us to partner with them to fulfill their calling and purpose for ministry in South Hayward. We were prepared to receive the torch and bring viable ministry to South Hayward's changing community.

After gathering and making copies of the petitions, we found the address of all the board members and overnighted the petitions with a cover letter about the potential partnership. The overnight delivery was guaranteed by 10:00 am—one hour before the call with the board.

Like Nehemiah who went before the king, all of Glad Tidings was in prayer that morning, asking the Lord to grant our petition and give us favor in the deliberation. By early afternoon, I received a phone call. Rev. Sands informed me that the board members had received our proposal moments before their meeting and voted overwhelmingly in our favor. Although our offer was the lowest of all of the offers they received, through the grace of God, our offer was accepted. It wasn't about money—it was about ministry and God's will for that community.

Today, as I look back at all the miracles and ministry and thousands of lives that have been changed, I realize that on the day our offer was accepted, only God knew the future. I've often wondered what would have happen if I'd ignored the voice as I stood on the street corner, and we had failed to trust God.

I flew back to Pasadena to begin work on purchasing the property and was asked how soon I could have a deposit. I asked how much and when it was needed. Their business manager responded, "$30,000 down in escrow within the next sixty days." I assured them that it wouldn't be a problem. However, in fact, we had very little money. I had no idea where $30,000 would come from so quickly. I stepped outside their office, looked up, and prayed, "Lord, help us!"

During this time, Dr. Dorothy Exume, a foreign missionary from Haiti, was ministering at our church. That evening she spoke a word to our small congregation. She said that God led her to tell every family to trust God for a one thousand dollar donation to the church. In 1981, that was a large amount of money, especially for young people, but we trusted God to provide. Through the help of the Lord, there was one miraculous testimony after another of how God was blessing families. Soon, people outside our fellowship were joining in this great march of faith. Within a few weeks, we had secured the $30,000, and Glad Tidings prepared to move into our new facility. Our first service was on Sunday morning, April 16, 1981. While the sanctuary had seating for only 150 people, we felt like it was a magnificent cathedral!

NOT SO STRANGE

What have you heard the Lord say to you lately? How has He communicated with you? If our spiritual ears are attuned to God's whispers and shouts, we'll have a vital, living, transformative relationship with Him. God isn't an inanimate thing; He's a person—a living, loving, communicating person, and He delights to share His heart and His direction with you.

Genesis tells us that God spoke to Abraham (first called Abram, which means "Daddy," then changed to Abraham, which means "Big Daddy") numerous times. First, God gave him the grand promise, and He told him to leave his country and go:

> *"To a land that I will show you. I will make you a great nation; I will bless you And make your name great; And you shall be a blessing. I will bless those who bless you, And I will curse him who curses you; And in you all the families of the earth shall be blessed." —Genesis 12:1-3*

However, the years passed, and there was no child. Then, in one of the most dramatic events recorded in the Bible, God reaffirmed His promise to Abraham, who was so discouraged by the delay in God fulfilling His promise of an heir that he planned to give his inheritance to a nephew. God answered by telling him to go outside at night and look at the myriad of stars: "Look now toward heaven, and count the stars if you are able to number them. So shall your descendants be" (Genesis 15:5). But God wasn't through.

Earlier in the chapter, I mentioned that God speaks to us through the Scriptures, the Holy Spirit's promptings, other believers, and the teaching of the Word. However, that's not an exhaustive list. God sometimes communicates to us through dreams and visions. He instructed Abraham to cut up several animals and place them in two rows. God sent him into a deep sleep, and then God showed up as "a smoking oven and a burning torch" and passed between the pieces. This was an extraordinary message because in ancient times, when covenants between two people were made, they didn't have written contracts—they acted out the punishment for failure to follow the rules of the covenant. Always, the *lesser* acted out the punishment. We can imagine Abraham fully expected that God would tell him to walk between the pieces of the sacrifice, but God, in the form of the smoking oven and burning torch, walked between them! This was God saying, "Even if you don't live up to the covenant, I'll pay the price." And that's exactly what happened hundreds of years later when God, in the form of Jesus on the cross, paid the price for our failure to live up to the covenant.

That night in the vision, God spoke to Abraham to assure him, in affirming words and dramatic actions, that He is supremely faithful to do what He has said He would do.

The list of people who have heard God speak to them is long and varied. Moses heard God tell him to go to Pharoah and demand the release of the Jewish people. Isaiah was worshiping in the temple and had a vision of God's majesty and glory. God said: "Whom shall I send, and who will go for Us?"

Isaiah responded, "Here *am* I! Send me."

Then God gave him a calling that his ministry would be full of resistance and difficulty:

> And He said, "Go, and tell this people: 'Keep on hearing, but do not understand; Keep on seeing, but do not perceive.' Make the heart of this people dull, And their ears heavy, And shut their eyes; Lest they see with their eyes, And hear with their ears, And understand with their heart, And return and be healed." —Isaiah 6:9-10

Centuries later, Jesus heard God the Father speak words of assurance. Jesus went to His cousin John to be baptized. Matthew tells us:

> When He had been baptized, Jesus came up immediately from the water; and behold, the heavens were opened to Him, and He saw the Spirit of God descending like a dove and alighting upon Him. And suddenly a voice came from heaven, saying, "This is My beloved Son, in whom I am well pleased." —Matthew 3:16-17

The writer to the Hebrews began his sermon (the only recorded complete sermon in the New Testament) with a brief history of God's personal communication:

> *God, who at various times and in various ways spoke in time past to the fathers by the prophets, has in these last days spoken to us by His Son, whom He has appointed heir of all things, through whom also He made the worlds; who being the brightness of His glory and the express image of His person, and upholding all things by the word of His power, when He had by Himself purged our sins, sat down at the right hand of the Majesty on high. —Hebrews 1:1-3*

After Jesus was crucified and raised from the dead, God spoke to Saul (who became Paul) on the road to Damascus, to Philip when the Ethiopian eunuch was approaching, and to Peter when Cornelius came to Joppa to ask how to know God. Today, God is still speaking. In his book, *Hearing God*, professor Dallas Willard remarked, "God's presence is everywhere around us. God is able to penetrate, intertwine himself within the fibers of the human self in such a way that those who are enveloped in His loving companionship will never be alone."[3]

God often speaks to us to expand our vision, broaden our borders, and give us hope for genuine change. At one point in the life of our church, I'd been preaching my heart out each service and leading in the direction I'd sensed God wanted us to go. A dear elder of our church drove twenty-five miles every week from San Jose to Hayward. One Sunday he came up to me and said, "Pastor, I've been listening to you preach, and the Lord laid it on my heart to get you a truck for His church. I'm going to bring it to you on Tuesday."

I wasn't sure how to respond. I didn't know I needed a truck, but I guess the Lord did. On Tuesday afternoon, the elder drove into our parking lot in a twenty-four-foot long U-Haul truck. When he got out, I shook my head and asked, "Brother, can't you find a smaller truck?"

---

3 Dallas Willard, *Hearing God* (Downers Grove: Intervarsity Press, 2012), 59.

He smiled and remarked, "This is the one God told me to buy. God bless you, Pastor. See you later." He handed me the keys and the title, and he left in a car that had followed him to the church.

After he was gone, I called Deacon Galloway and told him, "I'm going out of town. Please hide this truck before the rest of our members see it!"

A few hours later, I was on a plane to Memphis, Tennessee, to preach for Bishop J. O. Patterson, Sr. I had a row all to myself, and I was deep in thought. I was wondering what I was going to do with that big, ugly truck. I felt a nudge at my side, but there was no one there. Was it a cramp? Had I dropped something that was poking me? No, it was God getting my attention. In my spirit I heard Him, say, *Your problem isn't that your truck is too big. Your vision is too small.* I began to weep. I asked God to forgive me for doubting Him and resisting this gracious gift. As I prayed, a vision unfolded in my mind and heart. I picked up a mental brush to paint in vibrant living color on a new, clean canvas.

I could hardly wait to return to Hayward. As soon as the plane landed, I drove the truck to a repair shop to have them make some alterations and paint it. A few days later, the newly renovated truck, now called "Friends on Wheels," was rolling out of the shop and down the street! It was radiant in green, gold, and white. One side of the truck had a panel that could be lowered to provide a stage for our puppet ministry. We used the truck to respond to mission needs and community emergencies with food and clothing, and it was decked out with a sound stage for other events. With the addition of a new, roll-out canopy, Friends on Wheels was taking ministry to the next level!

The elder who gave us the truck had listened to God's voice and responded in faith. I was a little slower to catch on to what God wanted to do with it, but He was persistent enough to get my attention.

NO SUPER SAINTS REQUIRED

We may think prophets and other extraordinary people are the only ones who can hear God's voice, but that's not true at all. God communicates with those who belong to Him, those who have been born again and indwelled with the Spirit of

God—people like you and me. I know of a young woman who wanted to get married to the man she loved. She was eager to walk down the aisle, but she sensed God say, *Wait one year.* During that year, God worked powerfully and deeply in their relationship to smooth out some rough edges and deepen their understanding of each other. She looks back on God's instruction to delay as the best investment of time in her life. Abraham would have understood perfectly.

God may break through to speak to us when we patiently and persistently petition Him to give us an answer to our prayers, or He may whisper to us when we least expect it. Like every significant relationship, there are unknowns and mysteries. We can't force this kind of communication, but we can certainly put ourselves in a spiritual place where we're receptive. Then, when God speaks, we hear Him.

CONSIDER THIS:

1) What are some excuses Nehemiah could have given for ignoring the report of Hanani and his friends?

2) Which of these have you used when it was inconvenient or uncomfortable to listen and obey God?

3) When have you sensed God communicate His heart and His will to you through the Scriptures?

. . . through the whisper of the Spirit?

. . . through mature, wise believers?

. . . through the preaching and application of the Word?

4) In each instance, how did you know it was God speaking to you (and not last night's chili)?

5) Does the thought of God communicating directly with you make you thrilled, confused, anxious, or some combination of these responses? Explain your answer.

6) What are some ways you can unclog your spiritual ears and put yourself in a place to hear more regularly from God?

7) Who do you know whose walk with God is so close that they're in touch with God and hear Him when He speaks?

8) What burden in your own life, family, church, and community do you need God to speak to you about?

9) Are you willing to hear whatever He says? Why or why not?

10) What is God saying to you through this chapter? What do you hear?

WORD ON THE STREET

CRAIG CALHOUN

Former Police Chief, Hayward, California

When I met Jerry Macklin, I could tell immediately that he is a man of vision and action. He was committed to far more than building a successful church; he wanted to create a successful community. He used every resource he could get his hands on, including the police department, and we were happy to partner with him.

There are more stories than I have time to tell, but I remember him starting a midnight basketball program. The games gave impressionable kids somewhere to go where they could have fun and stay away from the gangs, which were eager to recruit them. He led a comprehensive and collaborative effort—including his church, our department, schools, and local agencies such as child welfare and drug rehab programs like Project Eden—in the neighborhood to help people with Section 8 housing and many others. He knew how to use every available resource.

One of the biggest problems in the neighborhood was that slumlords turned their properties over to drug dealers where they sold product. These buildings quickly deteriorated, so the problems multiplied. Drugs were on every corner as well as in the houses, gangs intimidated people, and buildings were in a desperate condition of disrepair. The dealers drove in from their upscale homes in nice neighborhoods, and when Jerry got the community involved, his people sometimes picketed the drug dealers' houses in their affluent subdivisions. Needless to say, the pushers weren't happy with him, and at one point, they threatened to kill him. We helped provide protection for Jerry and his family, but before too long, he made himself quite visible to everyone in the neighborhood. He refused to back down. He stood tall and put even more pressure on the dealers. He wasn't against the dealers—he loved them; he was just against their business practices. He was committed to change the culture one life at a time and make South Hayward a place where people wanted to live.

Jerry Macklin is a straight shooter. He doesn't mince words when he describes a problem or when he points out places where authorities fall short. It didn't take long for me to see him as a partner, and we became good friends. I especially appreciated his presence at meetings of the city council. I often wrestled with council members over personnel, programs, and the allocation of resources from city agencies and departments. When Jerry walked into the room, I knew I had an ally. Everyone on the council respected him tremendously, so they listened when he spoke. I worked under the auspices of the city council, so they could follow my advice or not. However, Jerry was an independent leader who had proven himself over and over again. We became a one-two punch, and he wore the bigger gloves.

People in our department always knew they could count on him. He came by often, and his presence was especially meaningful when someone on the force was hurt or killed. He was calming and inspiring to all of our men and women. When officers had a chance to transfer, many of them chose to stay in the neighborhood, to a significant extent because they appreciated Jerry so much.

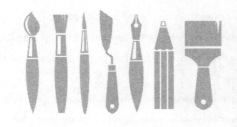

CHAPTER 3

TELL ME WHAT YOU FEEL

Nehemiah Felt What No One Else Felt

Sixteen centuries ago, a pastor in North Africa had an insight that has remained a cutting-edge spiritual truth throughout the generations. Augustine taught that the root problem of mankind is "disordered loves." That is, we love secondary things more than primary things. All of us have this problem: God deserves our highest praise and deepest affection, but we're often preoccupied with preoccupations such as power, control, popularity, and comfort (among other competing agendas). Vision is most clear when we are truly focused on God's agenda and His purpose and will for our lives.

What does this have to do with Nehemiah? Everything! Let's go back to the moment when he received the message that shook him to his core. The sad message he received informed him of the desperate and vulnerable people in Jerusalem. After he heard his brother Hanani, he described his instant response: "So it was, when I heard these words, that I sat down and wept, and mourned for many days; I was fasting and praying before the God of heaven" (Nehemiah 1:4). Jesus was often "moved with compassion" so deeply that the original language actually refers to his innermost being. That's the image we get of Nehemiah—he was shaken to the core. He felt deep anguish because he loved deeply.

When was the last time you felt such grief and sadness that it drove you to your knees?

When was the last time you wept over the heartbreak of something that you witnessed that shook your very core?

When was the last time you were so moved by grief or anger that it propelled you to bold action to care for those who were suffering?

A BURDEN . . . WITH HOPE

It is my deep belief that you must *feel* something before you *see* something. What you see is most often birthed by what you feel. Is it possible that we don't see more because we don't feel more? What you feel is an indication of not only what you will see, but what you believe, and yes, what you're motivated to do.

I know people who are impacted by what they see, but they have no hope for real and lasting change, so they soon descend into self-pity, blaming others, and ongoing resentment. Their hopelessness of what they see clouds their thinking and consumes their emotions. I also know some amazing people who view adversity and challenges with a bedrock of faith that God can do something wonderful even in the midst of calamity. The burden they feel serves as a lens cleaner, helping them see more clearly. Their deep burden births in a vision of the future—a vision that becomes more bold, more acute, and more compelling. They weep, but these aren't bitter tears. They pray, and their prayers lay hold of the heart and might of God. They don't ignore the often stark reality of the problem. Instead, they face realities with faith, patience, and a dogged persistence that refuses to quit or be deterred. In this process, they actually sense the burden more deeply, but they're not crushed by it. They trust God for a plan, a breakthrough, a resource they haven't yet identified and employed. They pray, "Lord, what would You have me do? What shall I paint on the canvas You've given me? I'm not painting what is; I am called to paint what shall be."

Our burden may be for a sick child, an addicted sibling, a rebellious teenager, an elderly parent, a jobless spouse, or a family dispute that's tearing it apart. Our burden may be disunity in our church, power struggles, and bitterness among those who claim to have been born of the Spirit and loved by the King of Glory. Our burden may be for the least, the last, and the lost in our communities, the racial animosity and political hatred that permeates our country (and our churches), or for those who are falling far behind in education, jobs, and housing. The list is endless, but I believe that it's impossible to be a thinking, seeing, feeling Christian without having your heart burdened for the people around you who are in desperate need. While you may feel for all those in need, you cannot answer every need.

What have I seen that has affected me most deeply? It's not just what I call out, but more importantly, it's what is calling me out. What need, what crises, what situation is calling me to stop, kneel, fast, seek God's Word, and pray for God's direction for my involvement? What is God calling me to do? What will cause me to say, "Here am I. Send me"?

As I seek the heart of God, the burden becomes the vision that captures me. The blank canvas is now before me. God calls me to say "yes," even before I know the details of the assignment. I suppose you could call this attitude a *predisposition* to do the will of God. The calling of Isaiah helps us see this most clearly.

The relationship of Bishop Charles E. Blake, the famed West Los Angeles pastor and former presiding bishop of the Church of God in Christ and the world-acclaimed and beloved preacher Dr. E. V. Hill is legendary. One morning in Los Angeles, Bishop Blake called the home phone of Dr. E. V. Hill. Dr. Hill, recognizing it was his dear friend, answered in his loud booming voice, "Blake, whatever it is, the answer is 'YES!'"

What would happen to God's kingdom agenda if our response to God's call was, "Lord, whatever it is, the answer is 'Yes!'"

Moses had a few questions before he said "yes."

Gideon had a few questions before he said "yes."

Isaiah said "yes" and then waited for further direction.

Nehemiah said "yes" in his spirit and received further instructions.

Today are you waiting for more information, assurances, guarantees, clarification, length of assignment, or job security? I ask: What's holding you back? What's keeping you from saying "yes"? What or who is preventing you from trusting God? Who has to give their approval before you move in faith? Nehemiah went to his knees in prayer and fasting, seeking an answer, and God birthed a vision in his spirit. Somehow, Nehemiah knew God always cosigns for leaders with faith.

Before Nehemiah had knowledge of all the details, he answered, "Yes!" Before he could evaluate the obstacles and identify the enemies he would face, he answered, "Yes!"

With every decision, there are "opportunity costs." When we choose one thing, we're saying no to countless others. I love this insight:

> *Kreisler, the famous violinist, said, "Narrow is the road that leads to the life of a violinist. Hour after hour, day after day, and week after week, for years, I lived with my violin. There were so many things that I wanted to do that I had to leave undone; there were so many places I wanted to go that I had to miss if I was to master the violin."*[4]

Today, many people enter ministry because it's their career choice, and others come to ministry as a result of an aptitude test. Still others have taken a spiritual gift survey and determined, "Well, that's it. I'm supposed to be in ministry." In coming to Hayward, what I heard in my innermost being wasn't a career choice—it was a divine call. A God-given vision always changes what you feel and whom you see. When you arrive at that place, you won't simply have a vision; the vision will have you. You'll pray, "Lord, what are you calling me to do about what I feel and what I see?" I've been captured by a vision. Paul expresses the depth of a divine call when he writes to the Corinthian church, "Woe is me if I do not preach the gospel!" (1 Corinthians 9:16).

Some might shrug and say, "I've been crushed, beaten down, and trampled by my own burdens. Surely God isn't speaking to me. I just don't have any energy for anyone else's troubles." I understand this perspective, but no one is beyond the grace, love, and transforming power of God to change us. There is no one the Lord does not love,

---

4 *2011 Pastor's Annual*, T. T. Crabtree (Grand Rapids: Zondervan, 2011).

and there is no one the Lord cannot save. Some of the most inspiring stories I've witnessed and heard are about people whose lives were so embattled they were near the end, but God met them in their lowest places and raised them to heights of new possibilities. You don't know your future until you know your purpose.

Not long ago, I met an amazing couple. They are the picture of success, but their story is much more complicated. I could see the glory upon them but did not know the story behind them. By the time the woman was fifteen years old, she had been so used and abused that she was depressed and had contemplated ending her life. Depression and despair almost won, but God stepped in to give her a new sense of hope that her life could matter—to herself and others. She and her husband married some years after her transformation, got involved in a church, and were discipled by an older pastor who helped them understand how to "live saved." That is, take on the kingdom values of Jesus to love God and love people with all their hearts.

They've devoted their careers to caring for others. Despite the man's very challenged upbringing in what many called the "hood," he became an attorney and entered the ranks of higher education and academia. From there, he went on to become a renowned college president. As the woman walked in faith and grace, she rose to the ranks of a high-level executive in a foundation that seeks to fulfill the wishes of terminally ill children. Like Joseph she was entrusted and given oversight and management of a multimillion dollar budget. Again, I believe this is a prime example of the many instances when God uses our deepest hurts to give us compassion for people who struggle in the same way we do or have done. It was only God who allowed them to paint on the canvas of a new tomorrow.

It's good to have sympathy for those who are hurting and struggling, but it's far better to have empathy, to identify with them so closely that it compels you to take action. That's the emotion Nehemiah felt. He didn't just feel sorry for the people in Jerusalem. What he felt was a fire in his belly, and a God-given vision was birthed! You know it's a vision when you place your canvas on an easel and begin to paint your tomorrow in vibrant living color. You must paint until you can see it, and then you must paint until someone else can see it. We say, "I know what the situation looks like now, but let me tell you what I see. Let me tell you about tomorrow."

SEEING BEYOND WALLS

From the beginning, God gave me a vision for beyond the walls of our church. I was sure God wanted us to have a transformative impact on our community—not just limited dabbling in the lives of people who had no intention of ever coming to our services. We would build strong, loving relationships and get involved in the structures that govern our city.

God gave us a vision of a community set in motion by His love and power, a dynamic that would change the face of a city and impact the world. This dream dynamic would motivate a growing group of young believers to a greater work and ignited the heart of a city in Northern California. The vision of vibrant and Spirit-filled worship would extend beyond the realm of the traditional church. Through innovative and challenging programs, men and women would be equipped to achieve their full potential in God. Through retreats, conferences, workshops, and seminars, singles, couples, and youth would experience new dimensions in Christian living.

Lady Macklin has grasped a vision for women's ministries that has soared beyond, even up to thousands of ladies in an annual conference and breakfast. Meeting one year at the Oakland Convention Center, the guest speaker from Milwaukee was overwhelmed at the sight of hundreds of ladies dressed in red. As she began, she exclaimed, "It looks like a red sea this morning!" The men's ministries and annual weekends have consistently challenged men to new levels of hope and accomplishment. One year, as they returned from their annual breakfast, the highlight of the day included walking the block in the middle of the street with hundreds of men singing in unison, "Amen, Amen."

God gave me a vision to paint on my canvas a church where people were loving each other and where we were loving God. At the heart of the vision was a special love for children and youth. This would be clearly seen as an outreach to future leaders and world shakers. Through the annual Youth Congress, drill teams, children's church, choirs, and other planned activities, young hearts have been challenged, directed, and redirected.

On the canvas, I'd painted a church that had acquired a reputation for promoting quality Christian education and hosting local, regional, and national conferences, in addition to Bible Institutes and training. Before I could see it happening within the walls and on the campus, I saw it on the canvas.

The question I am most often asked as people tour our campus is this: "Bishop, did you see all this when you started?"

The answer is always, "Absolutely, NOT!"

Bible study programs would give birth to outstanding Christian literature and workbooks that would find their way into churches and homes. The *Sunrise Devotional Journal*, *Foundations for Discipleship*, *Call to Excellence*, and other study material would be used throughout the continental United States and as far away as Africa, the Philippines, and even the Persian Gulf.

Bishop, did you see all this when you started? Absolutely, NOT! As the congregation grew too large for special services on site, the annual Easter services would be held at the downtown Centennial Hall Auditorium, where thousands would come over the years to hear a message of the resurrected Lord and Savior and enjoy the annual Easter cantata. Not restricted by walls, the arms of a community of Spirit-filled believers would share God's love through multiple outreach ministries. Friends on Wheels and Hands of Love would become a mainstay of the outreach efforts. Prison outreach would extend to San Quentin, Martinez, and Santa Rita County Jail, as well as the California Youth Authorities in Stockton and other centers of incarceration. Hospital patients and convalescent residences would be comforted and encouraged through an abundance of volunteers active in pastoral care ministries.

Bishop did you see all this when you started?

Absolutely, NOT!

After forty years of ministry, my perspective remains the same:

GO AS FAR AS YOU CAN SEE, AND YOU WILL SEE EVEN FARTHER.

Jesus told the crowd gathered on the hillside:

> *Always remember, "You are the light of the world. A city that is set on a hill cannot be hidden. Nor do they light a lamp and put it under a basket, but on a lampstand, and it gives light to all who are in the house. Let your light so shine before men, that they may see your good works and glorify your Father in heaven." —Matthew 5:14-16*

That's God's calling, not only for our church (and every church throughout the world), but a calling every believer should take seriously. It is our high privilege and our solemn responsibility to be the hands, feet, and voice of Jesus outside the walls of the sanctuary.

SEEING MIRACLE DOORS

In 1993, I was driving on Mission Boulevard, just north of Tennyson Road in the city of Hayward when I noticed a sign advertising a garage sale. I quickly turned right, and found myself in front of an older home with an assortment of items displayed on tables and in the driveway. Immediately, my attention was drawn to six large doors, impressive and stately even without the beveled stained glass that would later be added. It was obvious these doors had once stood as an entrance to an important office or building.

After one glance, I knew in my heart I was looking at the welcoming entrance to our new church. The fact that the project hadn't been announced, planned, or built wasn't a deterrent to the dream that was now so clear. In that "God moment" at the garage sale, a clear vision was birthed, and a critical link to our destiny stood before me.

I asked the person overseeing the sale about the history of the doors, and he explained that they had been recently removed from a prestigious law office. My next question was obvious: "What's the cost of one door?"

The owner stared at the set of doors and said, "$125 for one. $600 for all six doors."

I responded quickly and said I wanted to purchase them all, and within two hours, the doors were en route to Glad Tidings. We covered the doors in moving blankets and stored them in the garage of one of the church properties. I neither mentioned to the church membership nor to church leaders that I'd bought the doors. For a moment, I felt like Nehemiah, who, upon arriving in Jerusalem and seeing the devastation, said, "I told no one what was in my heart." The doors would remain in obscurity for months.

Then, in January of 1995, while I was facilitating our Annual Leadership Conference in the Santa Clara Convention Center, I felt led to announce by faith the building of a new sanctuary. I described my vision for the building, and I added the news about the purchase of the six new doors. That Saturday morning, I asked one of the brothers of the church to return to Hayward and bring one of the miracle doors out of storage. Like a treasure brought out of darkness, the unveiled door would soon swing wide, welcoming people from all walks of life. We call them "miracle doors" because people walk through them to experience the miracle of God's love, forgiveness, presence, and power.

Lady Macklin and I spent many hours discussing the design of the new sanctuary: circular, wide aisles, vaulted ceilings, and yes, six lobby doors. After we selected the architect, we informed him of our design preferences. When he asked why the sanctuary needed space for six entrance doors, we explained that the doors had already been purchased and were waiting to be installed. During construction, there would be a number of changes and alterations to the original plans, but at no time were changes to the entrance doors open for discussion. When challenges arose, and there were many, I often reminded God that the church had to be completed because He had already given us the doors.

Over the years, thousands upon thousands have walked through these six miracle doors. Yes, God had given us the doors and then a sanctuary that stands as a testimony to His awesome and miraculous power. As the years unfold, people of all cultures, backgrounds, and life experiences continue to testify of the miraculous life changing experiences that have awaited them as they've walked through "the miracle doors."

Let me give a little more spiritual background to the doors and share some of the reasons they mean so much to me and the people of our church. The doors I discovered at the garage sale were greatly undervalued. They had no permanent home and no designated use. They were simply being sold for the best price . . . or discarded in the next trash pickup. When originally purchased, the doors were solid wood, but before they were installed in the new sanctuary, a crystal stained glass window was inserted in each one to allow the light to shine through. The light that shines through the windows is a sign to those entering of a wonderful destiny that awaits them. It was our prayer that everyone would experience a new dimension in their lives as they walked through the miracle doors of Glad Tidings.

The doors remind me that our "members" aren't just those on the rolls or those who walk through the doors—a church's largest membership is outside the doors of the church. Those who are beyond your doors may not claim you, but that doesn't keep you from claiming them. Speak to your neighbors as if they are members. Minister to them as if they are part of your church, and treat them as family.

Instead of focusing only on the people who come to our services, I've taken the posture that I'm the pastor of every person in our community. (No, I'm not trying to take people away from other churches. I'm talking about the people who don't come to church at all.) I approach people from every walk of life and introduce myself: "Hi, I'm Pastor Macklin, and I'm your pastor. Here's my card!" I claim every pusher, drug user, gang banger, dropout, juvenile delinquent, parolee, alcoholic, and good, upstanding white-collar crooks. Without exception, I tell them, "Hi, I'm your pastor!"

Every person with a problem who comes our way gives us an opportunity to let our lights shine—an opportunity for people to see the gospel of grace in living color. I'm asked to preach funerals for people who aren't members, but I minister to them as if they were. Often we feed them, print programs, and provide music and ushers. We treat people like they're family, and they are. I've been asked to intervene with police and other city authorities, and I've treated their families like they were my family.

Through the prophet Isaiah, God invites everyone to come to Him for blessings. No one is left out. No one is outside the reach of God's love.

> *"Ho! Everyone who thirsts, Come to the waters; And you who have no money, Come, buy and eat. Yes, come, buy wine and milk Without money and without price. Why do you spend money for what is not bread, And your wages for what does not satisfy? Listen carefully to Me, and eat what is good, And let your soul delight itself in abundance." —Isaiah 55:1-2*

Today, a frequent discussion among ministers in this post-pandemic era revolves around how long we should preach. Twenty, thirty, forty-five minutes? The answer is, "Much longer than that!" Our message must follow people home and continue to preach God's forgiveness, love, and power to overcome, all day every day—not just for a few minutes on Sunday, but Monday through Saturday too. And it's not just the preacher who shares the gospel message in word and deed. It's the joy and responsibility of the entire congregation to preach the Word of life in their schools, their offices, their shops, their living rooms, and wherever they go. Let me put it this way: We're never *not* the light of the world!

SEEING ANOTHER CHURCH: "THE LEAST OF THESE"

I was in St. Louis when Councilman Henson called me early on a Tuesday morning in mid-December 2004: "Bishop, you need to get on a plane and come back to Hayward now!"

My mind raced with all kinds of possibilities that might explain the urgency in his voice. I asked, "What's going on?"

He told me, "A small, Latino church on Russ Road is scheduled to be closed today. I thought you'd want to know."

The next available flight brought me back to Hayward just in time to walk into the city council meeting. After discussions and debates by council members, I spoke clearly of my opposition to the plan and asked if I could intervene to resolve the issues. After all, considering the closure of a church two weeks before Christmas was grossly inappropriate. I didn't know the pastor, but the negative implications of failing to stand with this church would be catastrophic for his people and his community. The council agreed to my request and directed the staff to work with me to resolve the problems at Christian Vigilance Church.

According to Michelle Meyers, a reporter with the Bay Area News Group, and author of an article published in the *East Bay Times*:

> *Juan and Maria Cornejo founded the Pentecostal church in 1991. In 2000, they bought the Ruus Road building, which has housed several different churches over the past four decades. Complaints started about two years after the purchase, leading city planners to place restrictions on the existing permit. When the church failed to comply, the planning commission revisited the issue, and after a 4 to 2 vote in October, they moved to revoke the permit.*

Meyers continued her article by describing the December council meeting:

> *Christian Vigilance Church received an early Christmas present from the City Council: sixty more days!*
>
> *Instead of following the staff and Planning Commission recommendations to revoke a permit and essentially shut down the church, the council gave the small Latino congregation two more months to find a way to meet city land-use requirements.*
>
> *The true Santa Claus was Glad Tidings Church Bishop J. W. Macklin, who, along with other local clergy members—offered his assistance to help the predominantly Spanish-speaking congregation overcome language, cultural, and financial barriers.*

"I just know that we're better together. We can work this out. If not, the implications are tremendous," said Macklin, who is known for the network he built to improve some crime-plagued streets in South Hayward. "Christian Vigilance," he said, "is reaching people that no one with fixed-up churches has been able to reach."

Council members expressed faith that under Macklin's leadership, Christian Vigilance will make amends with neighbors. Some of them have complained for a couple of years about members arriving early in the morning and honking horns so someone can open up the gate so they can gain entry to church grounds.

Neighbors also have complained about unsupervised children making noise outside and music blaring through open windows and doors.

The council has asked church leaders to submit a written plan of action for meeting other physical requirements, such as installing a sound wall between the church property and the neighbors and repaving and lighting the parking lot.

"If anyone can do it, it's you," Councilman Matt Jimenez told Macklin.[5]

Juan Cornejo, the church's pastor, said parishioners left the hearing relieved, happy, and appreciative of the community support. Macklin "was like a gift from God . . . an angel," Cornejo said.

Over the next two months, I consulted with the pastor to resolve outstanding issues. At the February City Council meeting, many speakers and advocates—including ten pastors—asked the council to drop the requirement of specific hours of operation. Pastors called this regulation unrealistic, particularly in a troubled neighborhood that's safer and cleaner due to the church's influence. "The noise of worship is better than the noise of violence," I was recorded saying.

The backstory was that as Glad Tidings' pastor, I networked with more than twenty churches across denominational lines throughout the city. Our goal was to stand united with a church, predominantly composed of undocumented immigrants who couldn't speak for themselves.

The following Tuesday, our efforts resulted in one of the largest turnouts ever to fill City Hall. Hundreds of people from churches across the city packed the lobby, lined

---

5 Michelle Meyers, "Hayward Church's Closure Delayed 60 Days," *East Bay Times*, 17 Aug. 2016, www.eastbaytimes. com/2004/12/16/hayward-churchs-closure-delayed-60-days/.

the stairs, and occupied every seat and the overflow rooms. Additional security was called as members from multiple churches stood shoulder to shoulder in a charged atmosphere. The church stood united.

I asked twenty people already seated in the chamber to give up their seats to allow pastors, many of whom were expected to speak, to be seated. Although the mayor objected, the seats were made available to pastors who had been standing outside the room.

As pastor after pastor spoke in an orchestrated presentation, it was clear that any thought of closing a church wasn't in the community's or council's best interests. The board quickly rejected any suggestion of a closure because many council members pledged financial support to the struggling congregation in their effort to improve their facility.

Today that small church is one of the best examples of a well-kept church in the city. Once again, I'm reminded it makes no difference who gets the credit as long as God gets the glory. Leaders who want to make a difference must always be big enough to share credit.

Powerful feelings of compassion for those who are hurting are the fuel of good and godly activism, whether the hurting people are under our roofs, live down the street, or are on the other side of town. They're all infinitely valuable to God. When we pick up our brushes, we have a lot of creative options to paint on the canvas of tomorrow.

CONSIDER THIS:

1) Explain why you think Nehemiah was so moved when Hanani told him about the people in Jerusalem?

2) What are some differences between having a burden with hope and having a burden without it?

3) Do you think of doors as primarily a way to keep you safe or a path to welcome others? Explain your answer.

4) What difference would it make (or does it make) to see yourself as responsible to care for every person in your community?

5) What are some practical ways your church can go beyond its walls to care for people in your community?

6) What is God saying to you in this chapter? What's your burden? What are you going to do about it?

WORD ON THE STREET

ELISA MÁRQUEZ

Council Member, City of Hayward

I've heard stories about Bishop Macklin since I was a teenager. He had a wonderful reputation for his love and hard work to transform South Hayward, but I didn't actually meet him until about seven years ago. When I decided to get involved in local politics, he called to introduce himself. I was in the car with my daughter, and I was so excited about his call. After we talked, I turned to her and exclaimed, "That was the Bishop!" She wondered if I would have been as thrilled if the Pope had called me!

We scheduled a time to have coffee and get to know each other. When I met him, I realized he is even more wonderful than his reputation. His profound compassion matches his limitless energy to care for the people of our community. Others who found success have left South Hayward, but he has stayed. This is where his heart is.

I appreciate how he has included me. One day when I was at the court house, a person on his team called to ask me if I wanted to meet a visiting dignitary—Rev. Jesse Jackson. I replied, "Of course! When is he coming?" The answer was, "He's here." That's Bishop Macklin—you never know when you'll get a call to join him in doing something special.

In my role in city government, I've seen his incredible skill in relating to officials in every level of the city and county to be sure the people in his neighborhood get the services they need. Recently, during the Covid pandemic, he has gone above and beyond to secure testing, vaccinations, food distribution, and other assistance. When others don't have a voice, he speaks for them. He does more than simply secure resources. He does that, but *after* he listens patiently to people, so they feel understood and loved. That's what I appreciate most about him: he's an activist who steps in to provide for those he loves.

Bishop Macklin is a master at relating to city officials. For instance, he has met with me many times to "run an idea past" me, planting a seed and letting it germinate before he presents a formal proposal to the council. For every project, he knows who to contact, and he knows how the system works. He's very strategic in going to the right person for the best advice and necessary resources. He has earned the respect of everyone I know.

One day he called on a Thursday to ask me for assistance. His church was hosting a funeral for a prominent member of the community on the following Monday, and he had a problem. The name of the street in front of the church had been changed from Forselles Street to Glad Tidings Way, but the change hadn't been registered in Google Maps, Waze, and other GPS apps. He asked if I could fix the problem before the funeral, so people from out of town could find the church. I told him, "The city controls GPS applications for our use, but I don't know if we have any interface with the driving apps. I'll give it a shot and see what I can do." Actually, one of our staff members was able to contact Google and make the change, so no one got lost coming to the funeral.

Today, civic discourse is often tense, and even hostile. I get calls and emails from people who demand that I or the council do what they want. Bishop Macklin never demands, manipulates, or threatens. He communicates very clearly, but always with a tone of kindness and respect. People are glad to work with him on projects great and small because he treats us like beloved family members. I wish everyone were like him.

CHAPTER 4

MINISTRY IS RISKY BUSINESS

Nehemiah Risked What No One Else Was Willing to Risk

I believe human beings are deeply flawed, but we excel at one thing: finding excuses to avoid responsibility. We're masters at denial and deflection, and we look for easy outs. Our most common strategies are insisting a problem or a failure is no big deal and doesn't deserve our attention and energy. We blame others, so we skate any burden to act and simply ignore the problem and hope it will go away.

A God-inspired vision—for our own futures, families, churches, and communities—is always about change, and change always involves a measure of risk. The status quo is seldom changed without risk-takers. Failure, rejection, and discouragement always loom around the next corner. When these obstacles rise higher in our hearts than the gain we anticipate from the fulfillment of the vision, we are tempted to stop, bail out, and seek ways to reduce the risk. To face these risks, it takes courage to take the next step . . . and the next . . . and the next.

After Nehemiah heard the distressing report and felt compassion for the people of Jerusalem, he came to a crossroads. Would he just feel sorry for them and promise to pray for them, or would he place himself at risk and do something about it? Let's look in on the scene:

And it came to pass in the month of Nisan, in the twentieth year of King Artaxerxes, when wine was before him, that I took the wine and gave it to the king. Now I had never been sad in his presence before. Therefore the king said to me, "Why is your face sad, since you are not sick? This is nothing but sorrow of heart."

So I became dreadfully afraid, and said to the king, "May the king live forever! Why should my face not be sad, when the city, the place of my fathers' tombs, lies waste, and its gates are burned with fire?"

Then the king said to me, "What do you request?"

So I prayed to the God of heaven. And I said to the king, "If it pleases the king, and if your servant has found favor in your sight, I ask that you send me to Judah, to the city of my fathers' tombs, that I may rebuild it." —Nehemiah 2:1-5

We need to understand the risk and the price Nehemiah was willing to pay at this moment. Through his integrity and talent, he had risen to the inner circle of the most powerful man on the planet. Some speculate that the role of the cupbearer also involved keeping the king's appointment schedule. (Did his robe have a pocket for his iPhone?) He could have concluded, I can do the most good here in this role. It would be crazy for me to throw all this away for people who hate the king! Besides, nobody could do this job as well as I can. The king needs me.

We sometimes have the idea that people we read about in the Bible are somehow made of a different substance than we are. We can see Abraham, Moses, David, and Nehemiah as characters who step out of The Avengers movies, incredibly strong and totally fearless, but all of these people were just like us. Notice that Nehemiah's countenance was affected by his compassion for the people suffering in Jerusalem. He didn't "put on a happy face" in front of the king. And when the king asked him what was wrong, Nehemiah was "dreadfully afraid." That sounds a lot like you and me, doesn't it? He decided to speak the truth to the king about the plight of the Jews. He said, "Why should I not be sad when my people are suffering so much!"

Then the king—a get-it-done guy if there ever was one—asked, "What do you request?"

This was the moment of truth. Would Nehemiah bail out and say, "Oh, nothing. They'll figure it out on their own"? Or would he say, "Why don't you send Hanani with some supplies?" In that moment, in the blink of an eye in the middle of this conversation, Nehemiah shot up a prayer for wisdom and clarity, and he asked the king for the moon! "Send me, and give me the resources I need to rebuild the city." While it appears that Nehemiah's responded in the moment, a closer look tells us more. Forty-two days had passed since Nehemiah had heard the news of Jerusalem's condition, but these days were not lost. As Nehemiah daily went into prayer, fasting, and consecration before the Lord, his tears watered the soil from whence a risk would be taken and a vision would be born.

The seconds before the king's response must have seemed like an eternity. Would he laugh, would he mock the people he had defeated, or would he enter into dialogue with Nehemiah? It was all on the line:

» What risk was Nehemiah taking in his career? Was it going to be over?
» What risk was he taking in his relationship with the king? Would Nehemiah lose the king's respect?
» What risk was he taking with the rest of the king's entourage? Would they despise him for planning to leave the luxury and prestige of the court?
» What risk was he taking when he arrived in Jerusalem? Would the people there follow a man who had been at the right hand of the king they despised?

Nehemiah didn't pause and say, "King, I really want to go to Jerusalem and address the problem, but first, let me take a good look at my 401k to see if I can afford it." Neither did he say, "Let me fast and pray for a couple of weeks, and I'll get back to you with my request." And he didn't ask the king, "Hey, I'm going, but if this gig doesn't work out, can I have my old job back?" From what we can tell, Nehemiah didn't have a backup plan. He was "all in," and the prospect scared him.

Fear gets a bad name among most people. Yes, every time an angel appears in the Bible, his first words are "Fear not!" I'm well aware that fear can cripple us, consume us, and render us immobile. But there are two kinds of fear: rational and irrational. We're less than sane if we're not afraid of jaywalking on a busy highway, taking control of an airplane when the pilot has had a heart attack, or seeing a child about to fall off the top of a slide. Certainly, there are phantom threats that aren't real, but there are very real threats that demand our attention. I'm encouraged when I read the psalmist's reasonable, balanced, God-focused prayer, "When I am afraid, I will trust in You" (Psalm 56:3). He doesn't say, "I shouldn't be afraid." He's honest about the feeling of fear and the very real threat he faces, but he rivets his heart on the greatness and goodness of God. That's where he finds comfort, assurance, and strength. Nehemiah took the risk, not only to seek a leave of absence but even to ask the King for his American Express card to secure lumber for the work of rebuilding Jerusalem.

COMFORT ZONES

Comfort is seldom a friend of vision. In fact, great things are seldom accomplished by people who are comfortable, who value comfort over progress. Our heroes are always people who pushed beyond their fears, who move beyond their comfort zones to do something that matters more. Dr. Martin Luther King, Jr. had a vision to achieve a more equitable and just society through nonviolent means. He faced the worst white Southern society could throw at him: bombings, imprisonment, mockery, and constant threats to himself and his family. He observed, "The ultimate measure of a man is not where he stands in moments of comfort and convenience, but where he stands in times of challenge and controversy. The true neighbor will risk his position, his prestige, and even his life for the welfare of others. In dangerous valleys and hazardous pathways, he will lift some bruised and beaten brother to a higher and more noble life."[6]

In a *Forbes* magazine article about people who took great risks, Harvard professor Ronald Heifetz remarks that "if you make one real decision in your life, that's more than most people. Taking a real risk? Well, that's just a rarity. That's because making real decisions and taking real risks require freedom—freedom from the loyalties, expectations, and fears that inevitably fog our risk-vs.-reward equation."[7] We can make a long list of people who faced failure but found the courage to keep going. For instance, from 1878 to 1880, Thomas Edison tried more than three thousand ways to create an incandescent lightbulb before he finally succeeded. Walt Disney's first studio, Laugh-O-Gram, went bankrupt in 1923, but he launched his new studio to promote his drawings of a certain little mouse. In 1984, Steve Jobs risked everything he had in a bet on a small, portable Macintosh. It's not too much to say that every

---

6 Martin Luther King, Jr., *Strength to Love* (Fortress Press, 2010), Chapter 3.

7 "The Greatest Risks They Ever Took," *Forbes*, 21 Jan. 2010, https://www.forbes.com/2010/01/20/greatest-risk-they-took-entrepreneurs-management-risk.html?sh=4201f65d3b2b.

person who has seen success was willing to take significant risks. They were willing to fail as the price of learning how to succeed.

Comfort zones are very attractive, but they're a desert where visions go to die. We might wonder:

- » Why are comfort zones so unproductive?
- » How do they kill a bold vision?
- » How do they normalize mediocrity?
- » How do they distract us from what's most important?
- » How do they erode our energy and expectancy?

If Dr. King hadn't been laser-focused on civil rights, it's likely the Civil Rights Bill and the Voting Rights Bill would have been delayed by years—if not decades.

If the founders of our country hadn't found the courage to declare independence, we might still be British today.

If Abraham had stayed at home in Ur, and if he'd bailed out on God's promise during the long delay, God would have found someone else to entrust with His promises and power.

If Moses had continued his excuses when he met God at the burning bush, God's people would have remained in slavery until God found someone else.

If Nehemiah had remained in comfort at the king's side, Jerusalem would have continued to exist in disgrace, danger, and defeat. The enemies of the people there would have remained in power.

If Esther had remained in her place of comfort, she might have been admired as the most beautiful woman in the kingdom, but her people would have been obliterated from the face of the earth.

Each of us needs to ask the piercing questions: What do we gain by staying where we are? What do we lose when we refuse to take a risk? What did the rich young ruler gain by keeping his wealth and saying "no" to Jesus? What did the Pharisees gain by clinging to their power instead of embracing the Messiah? What did Judas gain by trading Jesus for thirty pieces of silver?

And what will you gain by staying where you are?

Another piercing question is not what happens to you when you remain in your place of comfort but instead how you impact the destiny of others when you, for whatever good reason, choose to remain in your comfort zone.

How much longer will people suffer because you choose comfort?

How long will darkness prevail because you choose comfort?

How will the future of others be impacted because of your need to remain in a place of comfort without risk?

A vision is just a wish or a dream when it's not propelled into reality by faith and bold action. Nehemiah wasn't content to just have knowledge about the condition of God's people in his homeland. Feeling deeply passionate was not enough. A real visionary is driven beyond what he hears and feels—he's compelled to right wrongs, fix problems, and realize change. The job description of a visionary is one who is willing to risk, take action, and compel others to do the same.

NO ONE KNOWS YOUR NAME

For those in ministry, one of the ways to tell if we're holding up in our comfort zone is to see how many people we know who aren't members of the church . . . and in fact, aren't members of God's family. Too many of us are content to remain in our "holy huddle."

When Glad Tidings was still meeting in "the Upper Room"—the fellowship hall of Eden Church—during the first three years, I learned that one of the world's great preachers, Bishop F. D. Washington was coming to the Bay Area. I called and asked if he would consider staying over and preaching at our third anniversary service on Saturday night. To my surprise, this legendary preacher, a standard-bearer for our denomination and megachurch Brooklyn pastor, agreed to preach in our rented sanctuary with folded metal chairs—not very impressive, to say the least.

Bishop Washington arrived on Saturday afternoon, the day after we received the keys to our new church on Tennyson Road. I was thrilled to show Bishop Washington our new facility. Bishop Milton Mathis, Superintendent William Peterson, and I sat in awe as this Church of God in Christ icon straddled a chair in the front of the sanctuary and shared wisdom, insights, and instructions to a young pastor sitting on the front row.

Bishop Washington shared a moving story of Bishop C. H. Mason, the founder of our denomination. For months a young pastor asked Bishop Mason, "Bishop, please come and see my church. I want you to see what I've done. Would you please come?" His requests were non-stop. Months later, after continued asking, Bishop Mason left Tennessee, boarded a train, and went to see the energetic, hopeful, and proud young pastor. When Bishop Mason got off the train, the young pastor met him at the station with a smile on his face and his eyes beaming. The young pastor was overjoyed . . . beyond words. When he and Bishop Mason arrived outside the freshly painted church, the pastor said to Bishop Mason, "Come on in, Bishop. I want to show you what I've done."

To his surprise, Bishop Mason responded, "No, after my long train ride son let me stretch my legs. Let's just walk a little." They walked and walked through the neighborhood around the square block of the church.

When they returned, the young pastor said, "Come on in, Bishop."

Bishop Mason looked at the anxious young pastor and said, "No, son, you need to close up! Close this building, and go up the street and help the other church up there."

In total shock, dismay, and confusion, the young pastor, with his eyes now filled with tears, pleaded with his leader, "Bishop, why? You didn't even come in. I have new carpet, new pews, and everything is freshly painted. Why are you telling me to close the church?" Bishop Mason responded, "Son, I've been with you now for a short while. We walked one block that way, one block this way, one block that way, and one block back this way. We passed a lot of people in this neighborhood, and no one knows your name. Close up, son. Close up."

As Bishop Washington told this story, it dramatically changed my vision for ministry from that day forward. I was determined that my new community would know my name. In some ways, it's a lot easier to become preoccupied with all the needs and demands within the church and let those things consume us, but God has called us to be beacons of hope to a lost and dying world. One leader observed that the church is a lighthouse, but many of us have turned our mirrors inward. The light inside may be glaring, but we shed precious little light into our communities. Bishop Washington's story about Bishop Mason galvanized my desire to get out of the office and into the streets and shops of our city. Our church began to grow, and our vision began to expand. It wasn't long before we went to two services . . . and then three in the morning and one service at night.

Ministry is not measured by the length of your aisles, the width of your pews, or the square feet of your building. Ministry is measured by the size of your vision. Bishop Mason's story prompted me to see myself as the pastor of every person in my neighborhood. I saw myself as the pastor of addicts and prostitutes, business owners, employees, the rich, the poor, the people who never missed a service, and those who had no intention of ever walking through our doors. It's not very important how many people claim to be members of the church, but it's very important that I see myself as God's pastor to everyone in the community.

My friend Ernie Morris, shared this perspective from his early years in ministry. He began his storefront church in Germantown, Pennsylvania, one of the most challenging neighborhoods of Philadelphia. Many people thought he had lost his mind to devote his time to the people in such a rundown area, but he had a burden that would be birthed into a vision. He had boxes of his business card printed. He walked up to every person he met—from business owners to gang bangers—and introduced himself, "Hello, I'm Pastor Ernie Morris, and I'm your pastor."

Many of them insisted, "You ain't my pastor!"

But Pastor Ernie smiled and replied, "Oh, yes, I am. I'm your pastor. You just haven't been to church. Here's my card. If you need anything, give me a call."

Many of the people thought about this challenged and forgotten community and concluded Pastor Morris had lost his mind. Gradually, however, he began receiving calls—then more calls—from people he had met on the streets. Pastor Morris claimed people who didn't claim him, and this kind of unconditional love made a difference to them. Despite what others could see, he set up his canvas and began to paint. He bought an orphanage in the Mt. Airey neighborhood that had been closed for many years and was in total disrepair. After remodeling, the church eventually grew into a congregation of more than three thousand. Who responded to Ernie's bold risk to initiate engagement with people? The people he called his parishioners before they ever came through the doors.

EVEN YOU

Lonzo is a man who has been a member of our church for years. He worked for a local plumbing company. One day when he and I were talking, I asked, "How much does your company charge for unclogging a drain?"

He answered, "A hundred dollars."

I asked, "How much of that do you get?"

He didn't hesitate: "Twenty-five."

"What happens to the rest of the money?"

Lonzo told me, "Well, Pastor, it goes to the owner of the company."

"Lonzo," I said, "why is it that you do all the work, and he gets most of the money?"

He just smiled and shrugged, "That's the way it is, Pastor. I'm just glad to have a job."

I said, "Here's what you need to do: Tomorrow morning, show up and tell your boss you're going to quit."

He reacted, "I can't do that! If I don't have a job, I won't be able to pay the rent or feed my family! What am I going to do?"

"Start your own business," I explained.

"But Pastor, I don't have any customers, and I don't have a van for supplies, and I don't even have my own tools."

"We can fix that." I pointed to one of our old church vans. "Do you see that van? It still runs. Take that van to the paint shop, get it painted, and have them put the name of your new company on the sides."

He started to protest again, "But . . ."

I interrupted, "Then come back to see me, and I'll line up a lot of customers for you."

Lonzo had enough confidence in me to walk into the office the next morning and tell his boss that he was quitting. He took the van to be painted, and he had "Alpha Plumbing" painted on the sides. The next Sunday morning, I asked him to park the van in the front of the church. In the service, I asked the congregation, "How many of you have drains in your house?"

Everybody raised their hands.

"How many of you have had your drains back up?"

Every hand went up.

"How many of you called a plumber to fix the problem?"

Again, a sea of hands.

I then told them, "From now on, you can call Lonzo and his new company, Alpha Plumbing, to help you. He'll do a great job for you."

This brief announcement launched his business. Lonzo later got his contractor's license, and when Glad Tidings built our new facility, he was our plumbing contractor. Alpha Plumbing also has been our go-to plumbing company for all of our facilities. Today, he's semi-retired, but he still oversees the business he began years ago with his multiple vans running all over the city.

A BIT OF A PUSH

Sometimes, it takes a gentle push and other times, an even not-so-gentle push to get people to take risks to improve their lives. Years ago, I used to see a man who was obviously an alcoholic, wander slowly past the church every Sunday. One day, though, he came in during a service. I was preaching, the power of the gospel was evident, and the man was saved. His name is James Tucker.

As I got to know him, he explained that he had tried out for the San Francisco 49ers, but after an injury, he had left the game and lost his way. He was living in the apartments next to the church. Because he was a single father, he and his kids were on welfare. On this particular Sunday, while under the influence, he had walked a little shakily into the back of the sanctuary. Following the message that day, James Tucker accepted Jesus Christ as his Lord and Savior and became a member of Glad Tidings. After about a month, he was growing in his faith and wanted to become more involved at the church. I asked, "Where do you work?"

He shook his head and answered, "Pastor, I don't have a job."

"What do you mean?" I asked.

He tried to explain, "I can't work because I'm responsible for my three young sons. I have to take them to school and pick them up every day. I'm on welfare. This is the best we can do."

I didn't pause. "I'm afraid that if you won't work, you can't be a member of our church."

Tears filled his eyes. "This is the first place I've felt welcomed and whole. Why can't I be a member?"

"We don't have any able-bodied men who refuse to work. If you want to be a member, you'll have to find a job. You can't just sit around and watch television all day."

He asked, "Well, what can I do?"

"What do you want to do?"

He thought for a few seconds and then said, "Maybe I could become a painter. I can paint houses while my children are in school."

I replied, "Sounds good to me!" I gave him fifty dollars to go to the Kelly Moore paint store to buy some supplies, and I hired him to paint the Fireside Room downstairs in the church. When he finished, I went to inspect his work. It was apparent that painting wasn't his strongest talent. He had done a terrible job! However, before long, another talent surfaced. We soon discovered he was really good at managing others who could paint very well. James would go on to become a licensed painting contractor, and he established an extremely successful painting business.

Please don't misunderstand. I'm not advocating that we take foolish risks. We need to be wise in choosing the risks we're willing to take, and quite often, that wisdom comes on the back side of a lot of successes and failures. Experience is a wonderful teacher, but we'll never learn if we don't enter the classroom. Nehemiah put himself out there when he told the king he wanted to leave the court and rebuild the walls of Jerusalem. As we'll see, he faced innumerable obstacles and hardships, but like all great stories, this one has a hero. In fact, there are multiple heroes: Nehemiah, for sure, but also God for His wisdom and faithfulness, as well as the hundreds of people who courageously rose to the challenge to do what no one imagined could be done.

How about you? Where are you in this story? Are you a Nehemiah who was willing to risk it all to do something great, to answer a call, fulfill a need, and shoulder a burden? Or are you one of the many who respond to a leader's call to get involved, and you jump in with both feet? All of us can take risks and see what God might do in us and through us. Don't miss out! These are big brushes and bright colors for us to use on our canvas of tomorrow.

CONSIDER THIS:

1) What do you imagine Nehemiah prayed in that instant during his conversation with Artaxerxes?

2) Describe at least three risks Nehemiah was taking?

3) How do you think our culture (including advertisements about products and services that promise wealth, security, and pleasure) affect the average person's willingness to take risks?

4) How do you think these cultural factors affect your willingness to take risks for God?

5) How much have you withdrawn from the world, so you can hang out with believers who think, believe, and act like you?

6) What would it take for more people to "know your name"?

7) Some of us are natural risk-takers, but others are more hesitant. Where are you on the spectrum? What steps do you need to take, so you can take wise but bold risks?

8) What is God saying to you in this chapter? What risk is He calling you to take?

WORD ON THE STREET

AARON ORTIZ

CEO of La Familia Counseling, The Alliance for Community Wellness

Bishop Macklin's son Jerwayne and I went to junior high and high school together. We were very good friends, so I got to know the Bishop from the time I was just a boy. In a sense, the church and I grew up together, and I've had a close-up view of all the changes that have happened in the community because of his leadership. My mother goes to the Latino church that's a part of Glad Tidings.

Our nonprofit organization provides a range of healthcare resources—including behavioral health to the schools and the community. In fact, one of our sites is on the Glad Tidings campus. The Bishop is completely supportive of what we're doing, and he has made connections for me with many funding sources. As he says, "If you're not at the table, you're on the menu." He has always given me a seat at the table, and I'm very grateful.

He has also consistently seen more in me than I've seen in myself. When the street in front of the church was changed from Forselles to Glad Tidings Way, he asked me to co-host the celebration with the police chief. I introduced Congressman Eric Swalwell, the zoning board supervisor Richard Baez, and Bishop Macklin. The mayor, the city council, and other dignitaries attended, along with thousands of people from the neighborhood. News outlets covered the event. It was a really big deal! The name change signified that God had done—and was continuing to do—great things in our community. I'm not sure why he asked me to be one of the hosts, but it was an honor for me.

Bishop Macklin often made connections for me with people who could write significant checks to fund our organization. He set up a meeting at the church's White House with a representative of the San Francisco Foundation. After the meeting, we received $50,000 for our efforts to serve former prisoners who were in the process of reentry back into the community. If it hadn't been for the Bishop, this meeting and this funding wouldn't have happened.

His advice goes far beyond funding. Over the years, we've talked about how to structure contracts, facilities, operational excellence, personnel, and strategic planning. Recently, he invited me to participate in one of his podcasts with noted leaders from the medical field. Again, it was a great privilege (and a bit of a surprise) to be part of that conversation.

When Glad Tidings held a church service to honor the president of Cal State University— East Bay, Bishop Macklin asked me to be the primary presenter. I asked him, "Are you sure you want me to do this? Other people are far more qualified."

He smiled and told me, "Aaron, you were made for this!"

When I got up to speak, I hoped no one heard my heart pounding and my knees knocking. Somehow, I got through it even though I was very nervous. After the service, Bishop Macklin came over and told me, "I told you. You've got a future in this!"

He sees potential in people when they don't see it in themselves, and his vision of a better future is contagious. That's why he has such a positive impact on so many individuals, and through them, on the community.

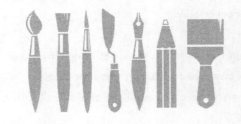

CHAPTER 5

STEP OUT OR STEP BACK

Nehemiah Did What No One Else Was Willing to Do

Action. Movement. Momentum. Change doesn't happen and visions aren't realized without putting plenty of skin in the game. Those who sit on the sidelines and watch can't know the pain and joy of actually playing on the field.

When Nehemiah told Artaxerxes that his hometown was in ruins, the king obviously knew that a man of action was standing in front of him. He asked, "What do you request?"

Nehemiah prayed and asked for permission to leave the royal court and travel posthaste to Jerusalem. The king asked, "How long will your journey be? And when will you return?" We don't get to overhear Nehemiah's answer, but whatever he said, it satisfied the king: "So it pleased the king to send me, and I set him a time" (Nehemiah 2:6).

But Nehemiah wasn't finished with his request. He knew he would need resources—a massive amount of resources—to accomplish the task of rebuilding. I'm not sure when he crafted his plan, but it seems that he understood that he needed the king's help. He boldly told the king, "To complete the task I will need your platinum

American Express card. I can't leave the palace without it." He was more specific in giving the king his list of supplies:

> *"If it pleases the king, let letters be given to me for the governors of the region beyond the River, that they must permit me to pass through till I come to Judah, and a letter to Asaph the keeper of the king's forest, that he must give me timber to make beams for the gates of the citadel which pertains to the temple, for the city wall, and for the house that I will occupy." And the king granted them to me according to the good hand of my God upon me. (vv. 7–8)*

History often looks inevitable from the rearview mirror, but when people make decisions in the heat of the moment, they never know how things will turn out. We may assume, *Well, of course, we won World War II.* But in the first part of the war, we and our allies lost every battle and were pushed back from every front. Nehemiah didn't have any guarantees that the leaders who would receive the letters from the king would give him enough materials, and he had no idea how the people of Jerusalem would react when a member of Artaxerxes's court showed up and tried to lead them. We know the rest of the story, but it's instructive to put ourselves in Nehemiah's shoes and realize his actions required enormous wisdom and courage. In the same way, our big decisions require enormous wisdom and courage from us.

A WORLD AWAY

The people in our community around Glad Tidings may live only minutes away from Silicon Valley, but it's a world away in economic opportunity. Many of our people struggle with unemployment and poverty, so one of our ministry assignments is to encourage them to move from welfare to work. That's not just an alliterative tagline. Having a job has the multiplied benefits of a stable, adequate income, a healthy sense of identity, pride of accomplishment, and hope for the future. Some years ago, the Lord gave me a mantra in my presentation to the people who were trying to move beyond dependence on government assistance:

Jump as high as you can, reach even higher, and shout,
"GRASP A VISION!"

STEP OUT OR STEP BACK 91

Make a fist, stomp your foot on the ground
(like you mean business), and shout,
"MAKE A DECISION!"

Now put one foot in front of the other,
like you are going somewhere, and shout,
"MOVE OUT!"

And I add:

"Come on now, start walking. We have someplace to go. He
who aims at nothing seldom misses. If you don't know where
you're going, wherever you stop will be alright."

When our people heard and followed these instructions, the room became a tsunami
of motion as people shouted and walked forward! Over the years, I've learned that
the devil minds little if we pray, but he works overtime to keep us from taking bold
steps of faith after prayer meeting. After we pray, we always need to ask ourselves,
What's next? What's my part in God's answer to this prayer?

A TRADITION OF ACTION

Nehemiah was well aware of the history of the nation of Israel and God's promises
for them. He knew the story of Abraham and the sequence of decisions he made.
First, God called Abraham to leave his homeland without having a clear destination.
Before he left, God gave him the global promise to bless him, so he would become a
blessing to the whole world.

Abraham and Sarah, along with his nephew Lot, traveled across a foreign land to
Canaan. When they arrived, God gave him another promise and some instructions:
The Lord appeared to Abram and said,

"To your descendants I will give this land." And there he built an altar to the Lord,
who had appeared to him. And he moved from there to the mountain east of Bethel,
and he pitched his tent with Bethel on the west and Ai on the east; there he built an

*altar to the Lord and called on the name of the Lord. [Nothing alters your life like
an altar!] So Abram journeyed, going on still toward the South. —Genesis 12:7-9*

Sometime later, Lot and Abraham parted ways. Lot chose the best land and pitched
his tent toward Sodom. Abraham took what was left. (It was sometime later when Lot
realized he had chosen Astroturf instead of well-watered grass!) God again spoke to
Abraham and expanded His promise:

*"Lift your eyes now and look from the place where you are—northward, southward,
eastward, and westward; for all the land which you see I give to you and your
descendants forever. And I will make your descendants as the dust of the earth; so
that if a man could number the dust of the earth, then your descendants also could
be numbered. Arise, walk in the land through its length and its width, for I give it
to you." —Genesis 13:14-17*

It's amazing what you see when you lift up your eyes. I believe God often invites us,
"Now tell Me what you see."

Years later, the promise of a son still hadn't been fulfilled. I'm sure Abraham looked
at himself and Sarah, now both far beyond child-bearing age, and assumed he'd misunderstood God's promise . . . or God had forgotten him . . . or something else had
gone wrong. He was deeply discouraged, but again, God showed up to encourage him.
(What do you do when God is silent? You remember what God said last!) As we've
seen, Abraham had been planning to make a relative his heir, but then . . .

*And behold, the word of the Lord came to him, saying, "This one shall not be
your heir, but one who will come from your own body shall be your heir." Then
He brought him outside and said, "Look now toward heaven, and count the stars
if you are able to number them." And He said to him, "So shall your descendants
be." —Genesis 15:4-5*

But still, no son was born. God appeared to Abraham again and again, most notably
through three angels who promised the old couple would have a child within the
next year. Abraham was ninety-nine, and Sarah was eighty-four. When Sarah heard
the angels' promise, she laughed. The Lord spoke to Abraham:

"Why did Sarah laugh, saying, 'Shall I surely bear a child, since I am old?' Is anything too hard for the Lord? At the appointed time I will return to you, according to the time of life, and Sarah shall have a son." —Genesis 18:13-14

And the next year, Isaac was born. His name means "laughter."

Nehemiah surely was under no illusions about the delays and struggles we who believe—even the father of the Jewish nation!—often face when we choose to follow God and attempt great exploits for Him. He could look back at God's faithfulness to Abraham as an encouragement to press on when times were hard.

Some of us have an incomplete understanding of what it means to follow Jesus. We think that if we obey, He will make things smooth, easy, and pleasant. I would ask anyone who is operating under that assumption to read a bit more of the Bible! The chronicle of faithful people in Hebrews 11 shows that all of them faced opposition, threats, ridicule, privation, and death, but they kept trusting God to do what only He could do. That's why they're heroes of the faith. When Jesus invites us, "Follow Me," where does He lead us? To marvelous miracles and life-changing experiences, yes, but ultimately, to the cross where the right response to His love is to give everything we are, everything we have, and everything we hope to be to Him and let Him sort it all out in His great wisdom and timing.

Through it all, faith is revealed in many ways. Sooner or later, we make bold choices to take action and trust God to do great things. Some people believe that if they have enough faith, God will do everything while they remain passive. That's not the picture we get of a faith-filled life when we read the Scriptures and see the lives of men and women who have wholeheartedly followed God! We should never pit faith and action against each other; they are a necessary combination of a Spirit-empowered life. They don't compete; they complement.

THE DUPLEX

Taking God-directed action inevitably means getting involved in the lives of people He loves, especially the lost, the least, the broken, and the disenfranchised. At Glad Tidings, we've had many opportunities to roll up our sleeves and make changes to benefit our community. One of them stands out as a remarkable moment in the life of

our church and our neighborhood. The duplex on the corner of Tennyson and Tyrrell was well known by everyone in the city but more particularly by those who live in our neighborhood. The building was extremely busy with a lot of people coming and going—almost like a grocery store. Some stood on the sidewalks outside the duplex, and others went in and out all hours of the day and night. Everyone knew what was happening inside throughout the night, as well as the day. Strangely, there was always a garage sale spread out on the front yard, the little bit of land with a grassy area. Anyone could stop by and purchase something, but an hour or two later, they would come back and trade it for something else. It didn't take much imagination to realize these were not-so-well-disguised drug deals. This went on for a long time, perhaps for a couple years, and the "garage sale" continued to grow larger.

We complained and asked the authorities to crack down on the drug traffic around the duplex, but they always insisted there was nothing they could do. The situation was becoming critical. Then, one day, someone knocked on my door. A police officer came in and motioned to me to follow him: "Come on, Reverend. We're going to the duplex today. We're going to shut it down. Come with us."

When I walked outside with him, I saw a large group of officers in full tactical gear. My gear consisted of a New Testament in my back pocket. (I felt underdressed, perhaps like David carrying only a slingshot.) We walked to the corner, and the officers went in. They found about twenty young men. Some were asleep, others were preoccupied, and still others were cooking something on the stove. It did not smell like dinner! It was really something else. Thankfully, there was no trouble, and the residents came out willingly.

The police put plastic handcuffs on everybody and told them to sit against the fence on the street in front of the duplex. It was four o'clock in the afternoon, and people driving down busy Tennyson Road instantly realized what was happening. They signaled their approval by honking their horns and shouting out the windows of their moving cars. Soon, even more people drove by, so the drivers and passengers could take in the sight. In fact, by five o'clock, cars had formed a long line to slowly drive by to gaze and honk because they were so overjoyed that something had finally been done about the 24-hour marketplace at the duplex.

When the police cleared everyone out of the house, the sergeant came out, waved me over to join him in front of all the men now handcuffed sitting on the sidewalk, and asked, "What do you want us to do with them, Rev?"

I asked, "Well, what do you normally do with drug dealers?"

He said, "We usually charge them and book them, but that's up to you."

The men sitting on the sidewalk realized they had only one chance to avoid arrest. Many of them whispered, and others shouted, "Pastor, help!" "Pastor, do something!"

I walked away from the officer to have a heart-to-heart chat (a "come-to-Jesus" moment) with the men. I said to the one named Dylan, "I don't want to see you or my brothers go to jail, but I don't want to see you use this duplex for drug deals anymore. Here's what I'm willing to do." He looked intently at me. "I'm willing to rent the largest truck I can find. When that truck arrives in a few minutes, you and I and all my brothers can empty this duplex. Everything inside has to come out—all of the carpet and everything else that's in there. I want nothing left. Put it all on the truck, every piece of furniture, everything that is there. I want it out! If you'll complete this job . . ."

He quickly realized this was a golden opportunity, so he interrupted, "Okay, I'll do it."

I thought it was both odd and appropriate to ask him, "Dylan, do I have your word?"

He nodded and told me, "Yes, Reverend. I promise we will do it."

I said, "Okay, then. I'll give you my word that I'll work with you because I don't want to see you go to jail."

I made the same offer to the rest of the guys, and all but one agreed to the deal. The large rented truck showed up right on schedule driven by the GT men who had come to participate, and the brothers went to work just as they had promised. (A trust was given, and a trust was kept. True to their word, the young men were freed from their handcuffs and went into the duplex to clean it out. They brought out all of the furniture and everything else that was in there—including what had been cooking on the stove.

They loaded it all onto the truck. When we were finished, I had one last word for them: "I want the best for you guys. Come on, you can do better than this. You guys are free to go."

I heard a chorus of "Thank you, Pastor. Thank you," and off they went.

After everyone left, I called the owner of the duplex who lived in Southern California. I had been trying to negotiate a sale with him, but he hadn't been willing to cooperate. He always refused to sell even though he knew what was going on in there. When he answered the phone, I said, "Sir, the police are standing here in front of your property. They just brought over twenty people out of your building." I explained that we'd given the men a choice to clean out the building or go to jail, and they'd gladly participated in the cleanup. I then told the owner, "I have two choices: I can send this truck to the dump, and we will be done with everything, or I can send it to the police yard, and they can use it as evidence. You know what the next step will be for the property owner. So, I'll ask you one more time, do you want to sell this property?"

He paused for a moment, then said, "I'll have my attorney contact you Monday. I'll sell it!"

I replied, "Thank you very much," and hung up.

To this day, I've never met the owner in person. We purchased the property a few days later and placed it in the name of the church, but that's not the end of the story. As Glad Tidings often did when we acquired a property, within three to four days, the duplex was renovated, painted, and landscaped. It was as if it had looked beautiful all along!

That Saturday morning, while we were working on the project, an older Caucasian gentleman from across the street walked over and introduced himself. He said, "I'm Gene. I've been trying to get something done with this property for a very long time. I built those condominiums across the street but haven't been able to sell them because potential buyers have to drive in front of that duplex when they come to look at my property." He lamented how nobody wanted to buy because of what was going on in the neighborhood. He gazed at the totally renovated duplex and practically shouted, "I'm so happy! Who did this?"

Somebody pointed to me, and Gene said, "Reverend, I'm glad to meet you, and I'm so happy for what you've done."

Gene asked if he could show me his condominiums across the street. He said, "If you have a member that needs a new home, I have the keys, and they can move in immediately." I wasn't sure what he meant, and he must have read my expression accurately because he then explained, "I'll take care of all the paperwork, and they can have a new house. No charge. That's how happy I am right now."

I looked at the young man who was standing next to me, James Tucker, the one who had come to church drunk, been wonderfully saved, and started a new career as a painting contractor. He had three children, was still living in the same apartments next door, and had been working around the church. I turned and said, "James, do you want a new place to live?"

He exclaimed, "Yes, Reverend!"

I said, "Fine. It's yours."

Gene handed the keys to James. He said, "Young man, you now have a new house. You can move in whenever you're ready." He explained that he would take care of the paperwork and that James didn't have to finance it. Then Gene looked at us and said, "God bless you. Thank you all for what you've done," and he walked away.

About two or three weeks later, the paperwork was finished. James and his children moved into a new condo across the street from the duplex.

Finally, calm had come to the neighborhood. The midnight garage sales were over. Peace had come—not only to the neighborhood but the entire city. Many people were clapping their hands and celebrating what had been accomplished. I'll never forget the sound of the car horns and the voices that shouted because they knew a change had come to the neighborhood.

James had taken a bold step to start a new career as a painter, and in the sovereignty, love, and creative purposes of God, had been given a condominium for his family. He was painting on the canvas of a new and wonderful tomorrow.

COURAGE, FAITH, AND ANSWERS

Some of us want God to provide all the resources for the vision before we're willing to take the first step, but that's seldom how God operates. At other times, God does provide all that's needed, but He holds the resources in reserve until He has prepared us, and only then are they released. Far more often, it's like driving on a two-lane road at night, and He gives us only enough light to see the next turn in the road. I've seen this pattern countless times in my own life and the lives of others who are following Jesus. And we're not alone. That's what happened to Peter.

Luke's account in Acts shows that Peter was, as Jesus predicted, the leader of the early church. He gave the first gospel message at Pentecost, he stood firm when he was arrested by the Jewish leaders and commanded to stop talking about grace, and God used him to open the door of faith to the Gentiles. Later, the apostle James was arrested and executed with a sword. Then, Peter was arrested. I can imagine he anticipated the same fate, but God had other plans.

Acts 12:5-11 describes how his situation seemed hopeless. People were praying for him, but they'd prayed for James, too. Herod planned to bring Peter out of the prison for a show trial, but before the guards got the call, something amazing happened: Peter was sleeping between two soldiers, bound to them by chains. Suddenly, an angel appeared, but Peter must have been a deep sleeper because the angel had to pop him on the side to wake him up! The angel told him, "Arise quickly!" Instantly, the chains fell off while the soldiers still slept. The angel then commanded, "Gird yourself and tie on your sandals." As soon as they were tied, the angel instructed, "Put on your garment and follow me."

Peter walked out of his cell toward a guard post. He and the angel walked right by, and then they passed another set of guards. They walked up to the iron gate of the prison. The heavy gates opened on their own, and Peter and the angel walked down the street. Suddenly, the angel disappeared. Peter must have shaken his head to be sure he wasn't dreaming. He said to himself, "Now I know for certain that the Lord has sent His angel, and has delivered me from the hand of Herod and from all the expectation of the Jewish people." You know the rest of the story. Peter walked to the house of John Mark's mother where people were still awake and praying for him. When he knocked, a girl named Rhoda answered the door. When she realized it was Peter, she got so excited that she ran back to tell everybody . . . and left Peter at the door! The people praying couldn't believe God had answered their prayers so far beyond their expectations, so they assumed Rhoda had lost her mind. Finally, they let him in, and they all rejoiced. (Here's the principle: Pray until what you're praying for is knocking at the door.)

My point in recounting this story is to ask a few questions: When did Peter's chains fall off? When he responded to the angel's command to get up. When did the way past the guards clear? When Peter put on his sandals and his cloak, started walking, and, yes, showed up. When did the iron gate open? When Peter followed the angel down the prison corridors, and, yes, when he showed up.

I believe God is waiting to free us from emotional and spiritual chains, to overcome obstacles and resistance, and to open iron gates into new worlds of opportunity. He's also waiting on us to respond in obedience to the commands He has already given us. When we take action in faith, God unleashes the power of heaven on our behalf.

Fights are difficult and messy, and journeys can be long and hard, but God provides a way when we trust Him. He makes a way for us when we show up. The spiritual principle is clear: Go as far as you can see, and you will see further. Go as far as you can now, and God will give you light to see further. What's holding you back? Your breakthrough is waiting, and it's in front of you.

UNPLUGGED

To accommodate the growth of Glad Tidings, we continued to go as far as we could see. We incorporated the vestibule (the lobby) at the rear of the sanctuary into the sanctuary seating. We then took the bold step of knocking out the sidewalls of the sanctuary to convert our office space into sanctuary seating. At this point, we had doubled the size of our sanctuary. We continued to go as far as we could see. We changed our service times to include worship at 7:45 a.m., 9:45 a.m., 11:45 a.m. and 6:45 p.m. We kept growing, so we began plans to build a new church, but we soon we realized the area around our property was unavailable. Hayward wasn't the only city with a neighborhood in decline, but we certainly among the worst. Our neighborhood was on fire with crime and drugs, and in fact, people were stealing from their own family members to get money to feed their habit. To ensure there's no misunderstanding, the problem was far worse because of the active participation of people outside our neighborhood, and the city didn't help very much. Like Nehemiah, we soon discovered that not everyone was pleased that someone had come to seek the welfare of the city.

There was only one property left in our neighborhood that would accommodate a larger new church facility. It was around the corner on Forselles Way. The building was in disrepair, but the lot was two acres. The property was owned by another church, a different denomination, and they weren't willing to sell to us. We were landlocked on our existing lot. The city was willing to work with us if we were forced to remain in our current location by granting variances. However, even with the city's assistance, the size of a proposed new facility would have to be scaled back and certainly wouldn't meet the growing needs of our expanding vision. The new sanctuary would only seat 350 people, but even that would be an improvement from our previous space. With no apparent options, we moved forward as far as we could see.

After we spent about $70,000 on plans and permits, and we had gone through the city's planning requirements, we erected a huge sign on our present property, right in front of Glad Tidings at 1027 W. Tennyson Road. It was a rendering of the new sanctuary we planned to build. The good, law-abiding people in the neighborhood were thrilled to see a sign of progress.

The Sunday night before we were to break ground, we held a trustees' meeting. Unexpectedly, someone knocked on the door. When I opened it, I saw the pastor of the church around the corner, the owner of the property we had tried on numerous times to purchase. The pastor hadn't come for small talk. He immediately told me, "All right, Reverend Macklin, we're willing to sell you the church on our two acres."

Do you think I was happy to hear the news? Not exactly! I responded, "What are you doing, and what are you saying? We've been attempting to purchase this property for two years, and now, on the day before we're starting construction—and after we've already paid the city $70,000—you walk in here offering to sell? Now that we've spent thousands on architects, plans, city fees, and permits, you show up!" I wasn't a happy pastor.

I didn't know what God wanted us to do. Should we say "no" and continue with our plans, or should we stop everything, buy the land, and start the planning process all over again to accommodate a larger facility. So many members had invested in the vision and had been faithful following the lead of their visionary pastor. I wanted to honor them and lead them well, but I wasn't sure what to do.

I told the church that we were going to wait, so we could hear from God. We had gone as far as we could see. We entered a season of prayer and consecration to discern God's will. In our prayer tradition, we sometimes hold a "three-day shut-in." I said to the church, "I know God will show up and give us direction by next Sunday." We prayed and fasted. Everyone was on pins and needles.

The next Sunday morning, it was pouring rain, but the church was packed with people on their knees asking God for direction. As I prayed, I sensed the Lord tell me, *Get up, go outside, and walk.* As I got to the door, some faithful men asked if they could go with me, but I told them, "No, you keep praying. I'll be back soon."

I walked slowly around the block. Fortunately, no one knew I was crying because my tears were mixed with rain. I didn't take an umbrella, so it didn't take long for me to be drenched. About thirty to forty minutes later, I walked back to the church. I took off my wet overcoat and walked directly to the podium. Like Nehemiah, as I walked, I told no one what the Lord had said. Every eye was on me. Then, I spoke clearly and forcefully, "Church, I've heard from the Lord. He is telling me 'Light shines brightest where it's darkest.' We're not going to build our church on this site—the site we've been planning for, the site we've invested in. We're going to build on the other property that has come available. Yes, there's crime, drugs, gangs, and even worse. And, yes, that's where we'll build with God's help."

When I paused, I was sure people would stand and shout praises to God for giving us clear direction, but the room was as silent as a tomb. It was eerie. After the service, many people who always greeted me with a smile and shook my hand avoided eye contact. Some just shook their heads, while others gave me a questionable look. That is not to say that there were not *some* who said, "Pastor, we sure are praying for you."

The curtain of gloom didn't lift right away. I thought, *God, when You tell me something, it sure would be nice if you told everyone else!* Then I thought of my father's words when I had complained to him about some that couldn't see the vision. Dad told me, "Son, if they could see what you see, they wouldn't need you."

It was a dark and dire time. I felt alone and misunderstood. I even began to second-guess myself. Had I really heard from God, or had I missed Him? Gradually, flickers of light began to shine, and God's purposes came into view. He assured me that we had gone as far as we could see, and now we could see further. He showed me that He was unplugging us from the first vision to plug us into a bigger, better one. We had to give up to go up, and giving up a dream is really hard. From that day forward, a new word came out of my spirit: *Don't marry buildings; marry Jesus.* Again, God didn't give me these insights before He asked me to obey Him and announce that our plans were changing. They came only after the step of obedience. Even with this insight, God's leading still didn't make sense to a lot of people. A number of people were afraid that they would be in danger going and coming from church, that the criminals would steal us blind, and our attendance would precipitously decline. Those were all valid concerns, but God had spoken. We were shifting our presence to the worst part of the neighborhood . . . to a place where it would be easy to shrug and assume, *This community is beyond God's reach.* But we knew that wasn't true. No one is beyond His loving arm.

The challenges of that neighborhood forced us to think creatively and boldly about ministering to the people. That's when we began purchasing, converting, and repurposing properties into havens of love, forgiveness, and hope. We didn't realize it at the time, but we were in the process of rebranding not only our church—we were now committed to rebranding our community. According to Dictionary.net:

> *Rebranding is a marketing strategy in which a new name, term, symbol, design, or combination thereof is created for an established brand with the intention of developing a new, differentiated identity in the minds of consumers, investors, and competitors. Oftentimes, this involves radical changes to a brand's logo, name, image, marketing strategy, and advertising themes. Such changes typically aim to reposition the brand/company, occasionally to distance itself from negative connotations of the previous branding. . . .*

The canvas was before us, and the painting had begun. We had gone as far as we could see, but now we could see further. No one started the work of rebuilding the wall because Nehemiah received a royal appointment and a specific assignment. The work began when Nehemiah showed up.

REBRANDING A NEIGHBORHOOD

Let me give just a few examples of our efforts to rebrand the community.

Spring Court

Directly across the street from the proposed site for the new church was the 32-unit apartment complex, Spring Court. The complex had been recently redeveloped and converted into two bedroom, one-and-a-half bath condos. Unfortunately, the owner couldn't sell any of the units. Every time prospective buyers would come to see one, either their cars were broken into, or they were robbed or physically assaulted.

One day I met with the owner, Dan, to talk about his problem. He couldn't form a homeowner's association because he couldn't convince enough people to move in

and purchase the units. I said to him, "Why don't we work together? I'll recruit the people to purchase your condos."

In the previous two years, many young adults had been joining the church, and I had been blessed to perform weddings for about fifteen couples. I went to many of those young couples and said, "I want you to buy one of these condominiums. This will be your starter home." I went on to say, "Buy it, even though the neighborhood is rough, and I'll build a church across the street. We'll work hard to turn the neighborhood around, and the value of your home will increase." I let that sink in, and then I explained, "You'll have equity! Enough to buy another home." To my

amazement, more than fifteen young couples responded, and all of these eventually purchased larger homes. They realized $200,000 to $300,000 profit, primarily because the neighborhood became a desirable place to live, so the property values went way up.

Prior to this project, when we'd go before city and county agencies, our people didn't have any real assets or vested interests in the community. With the success of the transformative development project at Spring Court, when we went to City Hall and the county and public agencies, we weren't just renters, and we weren't just passing through the neighborhood—we were tax-paying, anchored residents. As property owners and taxpayers, officials paid attention because we had become an integral part of the community's economic interests. Not only would I have a voice at city council meetings and a seat at the table where policies were hammered out, but now the residents who lived in the community could lift their voices and demand change. Unlike renters, whose voices were often devalued and muted, we were heard. Before, I'd stood alone as the pastor, but now we stood together as homeowners! We were tax-paying residents who could impact the direction of the neighborhood . . . their neighborhood . . . our neighborhood. This was real community transformation. With this relatively small change came a really big change, especially a change in mindset. The residents who lived on our campus not only cared about their property, they also cared about the neighborhood. They began to influence school board, City Hall, and community-policing meetings.

Banks have been known for a terrible practice called "redlining." According to the Fair Housing Act, "Redlining is the practice of denying a creditworthy applicant a loan for housing in a certain neighborhood even though the applicant may otherwise be eligible for the loan."

As God worked in us, through us, and around us, He gave us the practice of *greenlining*—welcoming everyone to our up-and-coming neighborhood. Today, in our society, wealth inequality is one of the biggest problems, especially among people of color. Our strategy certainly isn't the only solution, but it's at least a significant part of the answer. The quickest way to gain equity isn't to put a few dollars in the bank every week. The very best way is for people to buy property for low prices and hold it while the neighborhood is revitalized. Then, values skyrocket. That's what happened around our campus. Sometimes people remember the old days and complain about the drug addicts. I remind them, "Yes, it was bad. The property values were down, but we had the opportunity to buy cheaply and enjoy all the gains when the neighborhood turned around."

At first, we were convinced something had to change. As we took action, something was taking place. And as we looked back from time to time, it was obvious that something marvelous had already happened.

This was community transformation happening in front of our own eyes! As our voices were heard, we did more than talk. This was economic impact, social uplift, individual redemption, family restoration, and cultural recovery at every level of our slice of society.

Many residents in Hayward no longer identify Glad Tidings simply as a church—they call it "Glad Tidings Campus." Before we arrived, the United States Postal Service didn't want to deliver mail on our street because Forselles Street was too dangerous. Now it's called Glad Tidings Way.

Lancelot Court

Located at the intersection of West Tennyson Road and Tyrrell Avenue, Lancelot Court started as a promising concept. Eleven prefabricated homes were coming into the neighborhood. It sounded like a great idea, but the project encountered one problem after another. Eventually, the homes arrived, but the necessary prep work for those homes was always in question.

I went to the owner who was putting the homes in and said, "Sir, we'd like to work with you. That's our church across the street, and I think I can help put all of this together."

He blew me off: "I don't need your help. I'm fine."

He was sadly mistaken. Needless to say, the project failed, not once but two or three times. No matter how much money and effort they poured into the project, it could never get off the ground. Much of the work was substandard, and the new homes couldn't even be connected properly to utilities. It was a total disaster. The property sat deserted for a year or more, and then people from the streets decided, *Thank you very much. We'll live there.* People who had no right to be there became squatters and took over the property, and since the homes were open, they just went in. The development quickly became an eyesore.

Soon, every kind of illicit activity was going on. City officials were embarrassed, but they weren't the only ones—the crime-infested, abandoned development was a blight on all of us. Eventually, the city decided they had to eliminate the problem by demolishing the development and bulldozing the land. When I heard about these plans, I went to the city manager and said, "Sir, demolition isn't the solution. I don't know how this problem happened, but I have a better solution than tearing the buildings down." We argued for some time, but finally he agreed: "Fine. What do you want to do?"

At that point, one of the dear brothers from our Community Development Corporation, who had helped me on so many projects, worked with me to find someone who would purchase the project and fund the restoration. We couldn't afford to buy it, but we were sure we could partner with a buyer and make it work for everyone.

We found the right buyer in Berkeley, and we helped redesign the exteriors, from the porch and front steps and landscaping to the children's play area. We worked with the City Planning staff and prospective owners, and soon, Lancelot Court became a model gated community.

Eventually, Nick Rackinsini, a representative of the Clinton White House came to present the city of Hayward a prestigious award for the development of Lancelot Court. It also acknowledged the successful creation of Glad Tidings Arms, a condemned property developed and repurposed into creative housing. It was a great day of celebration.

At the eleven-unit development, it didn't take long for families to purchase the homes and move in, including one or two families from Glad Tidings. Today, Lancelot Court is still a top-notch project. Many people have no idea that we played a role in reclaiming and restoring this gated neighborhood. Thank God that He's always working behind the scenes!

From the Farmhouse to the White House

If there had been a contest for the worst-kept house in our neighborhood, the hands-down winner would have been an old, dilapidated, abandoned farmhouse.

The city had condemned it and had plans to demolish it, but when I heard the news, I offered to purchase it.

We did some research to find out more about our newly acquired old house, and we discovered that it was the oldest house in our neighborhood—it had been moved there in 1920s on skids pulled by horses. It needed some love . . . a lot of love.

If you've seen some of the HGTV shows about all the work that goes into restoring old homes, you have a good idea of the challenges we faced. Our people dove into the work, and that old house became our hospitality suite. It's so strikingly handsome that people from all over the area drive by to see it. We call it the "Glad Tidings White House." The landscaping is beautiful, and gas lights around the property remind people of a bygone era. The French provincial furnishings and draperies came from my mother's home when she went to an assisted living center, so it always feels very familiar and comfortable to me. With the stately white columns that adorn the front of the historic home, it's a source of pride in our community.

This is the place where we invite people for major events. If we need to have a meeting of city officials and community leaders, we have it there. We host notable people like congressmen, senators, the Rev. Jesse Jackson, and many others for lunch. At 10:00 a.m. every Sunday between services, the GT White House is open to church guests for an

executive brunch of the finest order. Those who serve are most often wearing semi-formal attire. There are no paper goods, only fine china, crystal, and linen napkins. It blows people away. They can't believe they're treated like royalty.

Joshua DuBois worked for President Obama as a liaison to church leaders. At one point, the Obama administration asked our church to participate in the launch of a new program, and we hosted Joshua and his team at the church and the Glad Tidings White House. After we ate, Joshua told me, "Bishop, I like this house! I'm going to send a picture of it to President Obama." I assumed he was just being gracious. He took a picture of me standing in front of the house. I thought it was a nice gesture, but I was sure it was the last I'd ever hear about it. Two week later, I received a letter that said, "Your presence is requested at the White House for breakfast with the President." That's *the* White House, the one in Washington—not the one in Hayward.

A few weeks later, I was sitting at a table with President Obama, T. D. Jakes, and other noted Christian leaders. Joshua introduced each of us to the President. When he came to me, he said, "Mr. President, this is Bishop Macklin."

The President's eyes widened, and he said, "I know who you are! You have your own White House!"

I responded, "Well, yes, I do, Mr. President, but it's not as nice as yours."

CHANGING THE LANDSCAPE

Business leaders and pastors sometimes talk about "changing the landscape" of their organizations through new policies, systems, or organizational charts, but we found that one of the most important ways to change a neighborhood culture is by literally changing the landscape. When you drive through upscale neighborhoods of any city, you see mediums with green grass, carefully trimmed bushes, beautiful flowers, and shapely trees. The message is clear: The people who live here value their community. When you drive through disadvantaged neighborhoods, the streets have potholes, weeds grow over into

the gutters, trees have dead limbs, and bushes that died in times of drought stand as brown sentinels of neglect. Where do you want to live?

When leaders have a vision of a better community, they can help create it by raising the level of appearances, and one of the best ways is by keeping the area beautifully landscaped. It says to everyone—renters and owners, those who have lived there for decades, and those who are thinking about buying there: "This is a place where people want to live!"

FLAGS, BANNERS, AND SIGNS

As the song lyrics say, "His banner over me is love." Signs matter. Gangs tag their neighborhoods by painting on walls to send a message about whose territory you're in. They have another message they send to everyone, but you have to be able to read it accurately. When we moved into this community, I wondered why sports shoes were dangling on the telephone wires at different intersections. One of the men from the neighborhood who had been saved at our church took me aside and explained, "Pastor, when you stop to look at those shoes, someone's looking at you. If you keep standing there, it means you're ready to buy drugs."

This clear, distinct message caused me to ask myself, *What could we do to send a new message to our neighbors that this was now holy ground?* New housing developments often mark new projects by erecting flag poles on the property's perimeter with bright flags blowing in the wind. Since it was our property, why not place flags on the street perimeter? I didn't ask if it was legal or illegal. I assumed it was better than tennis shoes hanging from telephone wires, so I went for it.

We purchased the poles, dug the holes, paid for the banners, and installed them ourselves. Within a few days, more than forty banners were flying in our neighborhood. Today, they continue to fly. And that's not all. Since the city doesn't erect decorations on our light fixtures during the Christmas season, we're more than willing to do so. No charge.

We soon discovered that permanent signs on buildings require permits. However, banners can be hung on your property with no permission required.

On any given Sunday, a pastor can preach a great message to 100 to 300 people, but every day of the week, the pastor can preach a one-phrase sermon to thousands by placing a banner on the building and other church properties. Most recently, in the height of the pandemic, three large banners were displayed on properties around the campus. They read, "We Still Believe God."

To this day, after countless thousands have driven through the neighborhood observing the signs, we haven't received a single complaint. As COVID 19 and, now, the new delta variant is upon us, our latest banner campaign encourages all residents to take necessary precautions: washing hands, social distancing, and getting vaccinated. Our campaign is called, "Let's Live!"

When you assume responsibility, you can offer solutions. Everyone in the church has a responsibility to minister in our community. Whether you attend the services or not, you live in our neighborhood, and we love you. We received thousands of small packaged hand wipes in conjunction with the "Let's Live" campaign. We're putting them in see-through plastic door hangers with an information flyer encouraging good hygiene, identifying the nearest Covid testing and vaccination sites, and of course, a note from their neighborhood church. Our goal is to deliver two thousand packages to the houses and apartments near our church. In addition, every Saturday morning for almost a year, we've served as a distribution point for 800 to 1000 boxes of groceries. We recognize the extreme stress people are under during this season, so we've erected prayer tents with volunteers offering prayer and encouragement to anyone who comes by.

You can't assume leadership without assuming responsibility.

FORTY PILLARS OF LIGHT

At a point a few years ago, the church had purchased multiple properties, which was key to the continued rebranding of the neighborhood. The words that the Lord had spoken to my heart as we embraced the challenge of community transformation were never far from my mind: *Light shines brightest where it's darkest.* The streets and the properties surrounding our neighborhood were noticeably dark and provided cover for all kinds of criminal activity. What could we do to change the dark streets surrounding our new church and the community? In upscale neighborhoods, the streets and roads have unique lighting features. The lighting brings calm and serves as a deterrent to unwanted behavior. Could that happen here, in

what many people had determined to be a throwaway neighborhood?God gave us a vision to erect forty pillars—six-foot-tall brick columns with large globe lights on each one. As we were erecting the pillars, we realized we'd found our calling card. It took two weeks to erect them. Our men used a powerful jaeger to dig holes for the foundations. Gradually, they began to take shape.

Like a musical crescendo, as each pillar was finished, they stood like immovable sentries on duty. On that last Friday evening when the work was complete, the church and the community gathered by the hundreds in the streets, and when the lights came on, there was jubilation and great joy. The impact was immediate. There was a heightened sense of security on the streets. And I noticed a sense of pride in the hearts of residents, as if to say, "Look at us now!"

We didn't calibrate them to be light sensitive and come on when it was a certain darkness because those in the shade wouldn't come on at the same time as those out in the open. We set them to come on simultaneously, in true GT style. Each pillar was standing tall and accented with a printed quotation. One-third of the quotes were from Scripture, and two-thirds were motivational quotes from giants of our past, pointing readers to brighter futures and potential waiting to be unlocked.

The lights come on each evening and bring light to the streets of the neighborhood, now known as the Glad Tidings Campus. The brick columns on the perimeter of Glad Tidings properties extend for several blocks and provide a clear signal that something new has taken place. These stately brick pillars have become one of the most significant campus additions and serve as a key component to our rebranding effort.

WHEN CHANGING THE NAME CHANGES THE GAME

After years of suffering from negative branding from the old street name, it was time to change. Everyone in and out of town knew our neighborhood by the street names of Forselles Way, Tyrrell Avenue, and Harris Court. Our neighborhood had been branded by the sordid history that preceded us. Even though we were no longer who we had been, it wasn't easy to establish our new identity. A newspaper article's headline read, "Pastor and wife seeks to change name of street." While there was some support in the city for the new name, everyone wasn't enthusiastic. In fact, many people were against it.

The process of changing the name of the street took seven long years, following the efforts of a small committee and one determined member who refused to quit trying. Finally, after several appearances before councils and numerous meetings offline, we caught a break. As a member of the committee, I had a consistent message for city officials: "This is not the same neighborhood, and we can't go forward with the same name."

In June of 2017, the joyous day finally arrived. The street was blocked off, balloons decorated the scene, music played, staging was set up, and festive activities were underway. Politicians and city officials shared speeches and words of hope, pointing to the future. As hundreds filled the streets, the new signs were revealed. It was a day our neighborhood will never forget. The worst street in the city's history was renamed Glad Tidings Way. It was a sign of hope and a vision for a better future.

THE LEAST OF THESE

For many years, about the only products sold in our neighborhood came in packets of powder or pills. Expensive, late-model cars came from other parts of the city, but after the drivers made a purchase, they drove away to their posh homes. Our neighborhood had a reputation for drugs, but the customers were often from the other side of town and other cities. Sending people to jail wasn't the answer. It was important to rebrand the neighborhood—for everyone's sake.

One day I noticed a young man who had been working the corner for a week or more. I watched him standing in a light rain, unbothered as he got sopping wet. The day before, I had asked some of the mothers of the church if they could fix a few hot lunches to go. I wanted them to be partners in my drug rehab ministry. They prepared soul food fixings: fried chicken, potato salad, green beans, and the trimmings. With a hot lunch in a Styrofoam container, I approached the young man, who appeared to be no more than eighteen years old. "Can I offer you a good meal? You look like you're hungry. You've been out here all morning, and you haven't sold anything."

At first he said "no" and turned away from me. I continued to engage him in conversation and assured him I wasn't going to turn him in. Besides, he needed to eat something. I opened the container's lid and watched as the aroma of the fried chicken sent a clear message of love.

The young man reached out for the box and said, "Okay, thanks."

I held the box out for him, but then I abruptly stopped. I said, "Wait just a minute. We need to bless the food!" At that point he bowed his head, and I went to work in prayer. "Dear God, please bless this lunch that has been prepared. Bless this young man, and Lord, keep him safe. Don't allow any evil to befall him. Protect him from dying on these streets." I continued, "And Lord, allow him to know how much You love him and how You want to save him. Lord, let him know You have a plan for his life. Now Lord, bless this food. In Jesus' name, Amen."

Churches can rebrand themselves and their communities through assertive, wise, and gracious actions. In *Generous Justice*, Pastor Tim Keller identifies three layers of assistance needed in disadvantaged communities: rescue and relief, development, and social reform. When a tornado, a hurricane, or a wildfire devastates a town, the people there need rescue and relief—immediate assistance of food, water, clothing, and shelter. Time is of the essence, so resources must be mobilized and delivered very quickly. Chronically downtrodden neighborhoods need leaders to step in to develop better housing, better schools, and better resources from city officials. But even that may not be enough. Leaders often need to advocate for a change in laws, policies, and representation to make substantive reforms in the social fabric. This can happen on a local scale, like working with community policing in South Hayward, or on a national scale, like the Civil Rights Movement under Dr. King and many others who fought long and hard for justice.[8]

---

8 Tim Keller, *Generous Justice* (New York: Penguin Books, 2012), 112.

REAL PRAYER, REAL PROGRESS

Rebranding a community requires a big vision and a heart for every individual. We need to hear what God has said, see what God has given, and claim "every place your foot shall trod." Don't look at your enemy and cower in fear; look at the greatness and grace of your God. Allow no one to stamp "veto" on what God has said He wants to do in you, for you, and through you. Go ahead and set up your easel and your canvas.

When we obey and act, we go as far as we can see, and God broadens our vision far beyond what we could have imagined. In the early years of Glad Tidings, I pummeled God with requests, "Lord, give me a church building!" But as we stepped out in faith, God gave us a campus with multiple apartments, a duplex, condominiums, houses, offices, and of course, our sanctuary. As we've worked to rebrand our neighborhood, God has given us favor to have an impact on the whole community. To Him be the glory!

CONSIDER THIS:

1) What negative outcomes could have happened when Nehemiah left the court to secure resources for his work in Jerusalem?

2) What was his motivation to press on in spite of the risks?

3) What are three or four risks you've taken? What expectation of success did you have? What guarantees did you have?

4) Do you think most Christians believe God often commands us to move toward darkness? Explain your answer.

5) Nehemiah, Abraham, and Peter all took steps of obedience before God gave them resources and answered their prayers. Where do you think their courage came from?

6) Who do you know who is a good role model of faith in action? What impact does that person have on others and on you?

7) What is God saying to you in this chapter? What is the step He wants you to take right now?

CHAPTER 6

SEEING THROUGH THE DARKNESS

Nehemiah Saw What No One Else Saw

Parents need a vision of what their children can become. In fact, every child benefits from three gifts that their parents give them: the gift of unconditional love, the gift of affirmation of talents and strengths, and the gift of a bright picture (a canvas) of the future. These gifts are important all the time, but they're especially powerful when children are struggling during the awkward teenage years or their dreams have been crushed by failure, the ridicule of peers, or the abandonment of friends.

I am so blessed that my parents gave me these precious gifts. Our home was a humble one. My father worked as a cement mason, and my mother did "day work" at Mrs. Blumberg's home in Hillsboro in the hills above San Mateo. While the work was difficult, a side benefit of her working there was that, as the Blumberg children grew up, we got the clothes they outgrew. They were fine clothes, even if they were a bit worn. Sometimes they needed a button or a patch, but we didn't mind at all.

However, Mom wasn't content for us to wear only hand-me-downs. Once a year, she took us down to San Mateo to buy each of us a new suit, but the suits she purchased were always too big. The arms on the coats and the legs on the pants were too long, and every year, we complained. She just smiled and bought the suits anyway. This wasn't an accident. It was part of her long-range plan. When we got home, she hemmed the length of the arms and legs and explained, "I didn't buy the suits for your size today. I bought them for the size you will be in a few months. When you're older, I'll let out the hems and lengthen the arms, and the suits will fit just right."

When I was about twelve years old, my father suffered a slipped disk in his back for the second time and couldn't return to work. The loss of income was a real concern because now we would be living on the edge. I remember my father saying, "We're not going on welfare. Somehow the Lord will bless us." During those days, we remained faithful to our home church. On Friday nights, the offering was designated for the pastor's support. Just like Sunday morning, as the offering was taken, people lined the center aisle to bring their offering to a table in the front, where their gifts were recorded. When it was finished, a deacon would announce what each family had given: "The Swindells—$5.00, Gills—$4.00, Claytons—$4.00, Smiths—$5.00, Macklins— no report." Our family didn't have two nickels to rub together.

One Friday night, before the deacon announced the offerings, my mother leaned over and whispered, "Son, take this up to the table." Reaching into her big purse, she handed me a jar of jelly, freshly canned from the apricots from our backyard tree.

I'm sure the look on my face spoke louder than any words I could say, *Mom, no! We're giving a jar of jelly?* Mom wasn't in a mood to debate. She looked at me and said, "Take this to the table now!"

I tried to argue, "I have friends here tonight!" However, the look on her face made her decision perfectly clear. I took the jar of jelly and walked to the front of the church. I hoped no one was looking, but it was obvious I hadn't put any dollar bills on the table. I prayed, *Lord, please don't let the deacon announce it!* I went back to my seat and put my head down. I hoped the Rapture would happen or the church would catch on fire, but neither of these events saved me from embarrassment. The deacon at the table spoke up, "We're a little short tonight. We need to go a second round. I'm asking all of you to dig a little deeper and give a little more."

I glanced at my mother's purse. It wasn't big enough for more than one jar of jelly, so I was sure I couldn't be embarrassed again. I was wrong. Mom leaned over to me as she pulled something out of her purse. "Son, take this to the table." She handed me a book of Green Chip Stamps, the kind grocery stores used to give. The number of stamps corresponded to the amount of money customers spent. I was horrified. I quickly realized that another attempt to change her mind was useless. I took the stamps from her hand and walked up to the offering table. Other families had given money, but our family had given a jar of jelly and, now, a book of Green Chip Stamps.

It was, I was sure, the end of life as I knew it. I would be ridiculed unceasingly by my friends, and the older people would laugh every time they saw me. But something quite different happened: God honored my parents' faith with an outpouring of blessings. A few weeks later, on a Sunday night, Pastor Alexander was dismissing church. My father was sitting on the front row, still barely able to walk. The pastor, who was my great-uncle, prayed, "Lord, as we leave here tonight, heal that man. Heal him now, O God! Deliver that man, and heal him even now!" Instantly, my father sat up straight, then stood up, and put his hands on his waist. He shouted, "Glory! Hallelujah!" And then a "Praise God!" rang out from the depths of his being like I'd never heard before. Suddenly, my father—who had hardly moved without excruciating pain for many months—began shouting and running around the church!

My father got his health back, my family got our father back, and the rest is history. All I could think about in that glorious moment was the jelly on the table. My parents never stopped giving, even when they had nothing to give. The Lord provided through that time of financial difficulty, and He used my father's physical healing to redirect him into another line of work. In addition to becoming an excellent appliance technician, dad would become the very successful pastor of a church in Silicon Valley. My dad had a canvas, some paints, and a handful of brushes, and his life was a work of art. What did he see that moved him beyond his past to a vibrant picture of tomorrow?

Vision doesn't focus on today, but on tomorrow—not on here, but on there. A vision is always bigger than what we can see, feel, and know right now. It calls forth our creativity and our tenacity. It's always a bit awkward at first, but don't worry—like the suits my mother bought us, you'll grow into it. If you have a vision for what you can do today, it's too small. A vision is not a self-portrait. It always requires the talent and resources of the Master.

Vision calls us to invest our time, energy, heart, and creativity. We're "all in." Visionary CEOs and pastors need to avoid the lethargy of too much contentment. But, you might ask, doesn't a strong walk with God produce a sense of peace and contentment? Well, yes and no. Certainly, we're content (more like thrilled!) that the grace of God is the sole foundation of our lives. And we're content with the many blessings He has bestowed on us. But leaders live with a nagging sense of "holy discontent." D. L. Moody wrote the following words next to Isaiah 6:8 in his Bible: "I am only one, but I am one. I cannot do everything, but I can do something. What I can do, I ought to do, and what I ought to do, by the grace of God, I will do." That's the heart of a visionary.

Every genuine movement—spiritual, political, in nonprofit organizations, or in business—has two kinds of members: pioneers and settlers. Both are essential for the long-term growth of the organization, but without pioneers, settlers have no new lands where they can move into and thrive. Visionaries are pioneers who are willing to go where no one else has the courage to go (at least not yet). Visionaries are willing to paint on the canvas of their tomorrow.

A young pastor invited me to preach at his church. He told me he wondered if I were like some other well-known pastors who wouldn't go to small churches. I assured him it was an honor to be invited, and I'd be delighted to come. As we talked about his church, he shared that he was believing God for one hundred members in the coming months. I told him I'd join him in praying for this goal. When I arrived and walked into the service, I noticed there were only twenty chairs set up. While I spoke, my mind was on the disconnect between the pastor's stated vision and his lack of preparation. I spoke for only about half of my allotted time, and I sat down. I could tell the pastor was upset with me. When the service was over, I had another message for him: "Young man, I've been praying with you for a hundred members, but I see only twenty chairs. I didn't come today expecting to see a hundred people in attendance, but I certainly expected to see a hundred chairs. You have to anticipate God answering your prayers and fulfilling your vision. When your preparation matches your vision, let me know, and I'll come back to preach again."

RECONNAISSANCE

Parents and leaders need to get a clear picture of reality as well as a vision of a better future. Without honesty about the current conditions, they lose the trust of people who don't buy into their "happy talk." Nehemiah understood this concept. He did an extensive reconnaissance of the condition of the walls, and he went at night with only a handful of trusted men:

> So I came to Jerusalem and was there three days. Then I arose in the night, I and a few men with me; I told no one what my God had put in my heart to do at Jerusalem; nor was there any animal with me, except the one on which I rode. And I went out by night through the Valley Gate to the Serpent Well and the Refuse Gate, and viewed the walls of Jerusalem which were broken down and its gates which were burned with fire. Then I went on to the Fountain Gate and to the King's Pool, but there was no room for the animal under me to pass. So I went up in the night by the valley, and viewed the wall; then I turned back and entered by the Valley Gate, and so returned. And the officials did not know where I had gone or what I had done; I had not yet told the Jews, the priests, the nobles, the officials, or the others who did the work. —Nehemiah 2:11-16

When Nehemiah arrived in Jerusalem, it wasn't the first day the city had been in ruins, it wasn't the first day the walls had been demolished, and it wasn't the first day the gates had been burned with fire. The city had been devastated for decades, and God's people had gotten used to it. Ezra had been given the task to rebuild the temple, but it would be vulnerable to another attack if the city didn't have strong walls.

Nehemiah didn't plan to call a meeting of the city council, and he didn't meet with members of planning and zoning to ask for permits. He didn't summon all the people to the square to tell them his plans and get them excited. He took only a few men on his tour. The route wasn't new to these men. They knew every street and every turn. They could identify the neighborhoods and where the gates had been. The rubble was so deep that they had to abandon the animals they rode on and continue the climb on foot.

After his thorough examination, Nehemiah was ready to share his plans with God's demoralized people. He didn't gloss over the problems, and he didn't promise a quick, easy solution. He was both rigorously realistic and powerfully hopeful:

Then I said to them, "You see the distress that we are in, how Jerusalem lies waste, and its gates are burned with fire. Come and let us build the wall of Jerusalem, that we may no longer be a reproach." And I told them of the hand of my God which had been good upon me, and also of the king's words that he had spoken to me. —vv. 17-18

It was that moment when the people were captured by Nehemiah's vision and courage. Before, their faith had been flattened under the rubble, but Nehemiah's vision (a canvas freshly painted) filled them with hope, and the end of verse 18 reports their response: "'Let us rise up and build.' Then they set their hands to this good work." If they hadn't seen Nehemiah's canvas of tomorrow, they may not have strengthened their hands for this good work.

Don't miss the significance of this turning point. When parents are both honest and hopeful, their children thrive. When leaders walk the talk, the eyes of their followers are opened. I have been a proponent of "thinking beyond" for many years, and I'm inspired by the statement: "Make no small plans because small plans inspire no one." Nehemiah saw the deplorable circumstances in the city, but he saw something else in his mind's eye: God's people working together to rebuild the walls—while rebuilding their dignity and faith in God. He saw them thriving again and Jerusalem returning to its former glory. Setting his canvas up, in effect, he challenged the men with him, "Do you see what I see? Can you look beyond the devastation to get a glimpse of a glorious future? I can. Come with me, and we'll trust God to make it a reality!"

In his biography of George W. Truett, the great Baptist leader, author Powhatan James observes:

The man of God must have insight into things spiritual. He must be able to see the mountains filled with the horses and chariots of fire; he must be able to interpret that which is written by the finger of God upon the walls of conscience; he must be able to translate the signs of the times into terms of their spiritual meaning; he must be able to draw aside, now and then, the curtain of things material and let mortals glimpse the spiritual glories which crown the mercy seat of God. The man of God must declare the pattern that was shown him on the mount; he must utter the vision granted to him upon the isle of revelation. . . . None of these things can he do without spiritual insight.[9]

VERTICAL THINKING

Nehemiah needed to be sure he saw reality very clearly, and he needed a few other men to be convinced that he saw their reality. A divine test exposes our default response to a crisis. Virtually all of us immediately react with a self-preservation reflex, but when the first blast of adrenaline passes from our system, we can think more clearly and respond with wisdom and strength. Change—whether it's planned or unplanned—is usually a crisis for a family, a business, or a church. Great leaders develop expert agility, so their wise response becomes second nature.

Believers have the limitless resource of the Holy Spirit to enable us to respond to life's difficulties. When Nehemiah first heard about the plight of the people of Jerusalem, he didn't seek advice from his associates. He didn't talk to the Persian HR department to see how a change of roles would affect his 401k, and he didn't consider Plan B for his career if this venture failed. All of *those* are evidence of horizontal thinking. Nehemiah prayed and fasted to seek God's will and grasp a vision. He stopped long enough to paint in faith on the canvas of a new tomorrow.

And when Nehemiah arrived in Jerusalem, he didn't let his observation of the devastation of the city cloud his God-given calling to rebuild the walls. He looked carefully, so he could see the problem, and then he looked carefully to perceive what God could do in him and through God's people to remedy the problem.

Life presents us with a series of tests, usually one more difficult than the last. The best way to make the right decision at major crossroads is to practice making right decisions at smaller crossroads. Practice and experience . . . they're wonderful teachers. The choices that matter most aren't the *hard* choices but the *heart* choices—the ones that challenge us to disconnect from secondary pursuits, so we can focus our attention and love on God and His supreme purposes. We often are minus clarity about our decisions until we take the first step God has clearly shown us to take. Oswald Chambers, author of the daily devotional, *My Utmost for His Highest*, writes,

9 Powhatan W. James, *George W. Truett, a Biography* (Nashville, TN: Broadman Press, 1953).

All God's revelations are sealed to us until they are opened to us by obedience. You will never get them open by philosophy or thinking. Immediately you obey, a flash of light comes. Let God's truth work in you by soaking in it, not by worrying into it. Obey God in the thing He is at present showing you, and in short order, the next thing is opened up. [10]

At every point of decision, we instinctively make some calculations: What will I keep if I stay here, and what will I miss if I don't take the risk? Faith is cumulative: with each step, we trust God for a little more the next time. Nehemiah saw God give him favor in his conversation with King Artaxerxes, and God gave him favor when he went to different places in the kingdom to secure the supplies he would need. Now, God gave him favor in the eyes of the people of Jerusalem, who could easily have responded with continued despair instead of hopeful enthusiasm. If Nehemiah hadn't made the heart decision in making his request to the king, he wouldn't have had the courage to stand before the people of Jerusalem.

FROM THE PINK PALACE TO FAITH MANOR

If anyone had asked, "Can you see the potential in that place?" most would have replied, "No, certainly not!" The 63-unit complex, known by many as the Pink Palace, was an eyesore, in disrepair, poorly managed, and a convenient hideout for all things bad. Drugs and crime took place in full view, with little respect for anyone, including the police or the neighbors. The units were townhomes, but they had been neglected for years. Police arrived almost every night, and shootings were common. The neighborhood expected little from residents who lived in the complex, and they were seldom disappointed. Moving in required little down, and rent could be paid in cash at the door with no questions asked.

It was a well-known fact that drug houses were scattered throughout the apartment complex. In 1994, we approached the owner of the complex, an older gentleman known for his business acumen and political connections. Our request was unusual, "Sir, we'd like to open a men's rehabilitation home in building 1001, #6. This apartment has been vacant for a long time and is next door to a known crack house. This unit is in total disrepair—holes in the walls up and down stairs, doors off their hinges, plumbing

---

10 Oswald Chambers, *My Utmost for His Highest*, October 10 (Our Daily Bread Publishing, Classic Edition, 2018).

fixtures removed, and pests and insects have the run of the house." The apartment was an unmitigated disaster. I asked him, "If we could remodel the apartment and landscape the yard, could we use the apartment without paying monthly rent?" The answer from a very cooperative owner was a resounding, "Yes!"

Immediately, work began. GT Men worked day and night for several weeks, and in a short time, GT Men's Home, called the "Potter's House," was open.

It didn't take long for six to eight men to find their way there. The journey to recovery through the power of Jesus Christ was released. New landscaping changed the look of the complex. Now, a manicured lawn and flowers greeted residents, guests, and neighbors. Those who lived in the complex were the most surprised by the changes. They wondered what was happening and what we were doing. Our approach wasn't to yell and scream and call the police to get them to move out. We had a different message for them: "The goodness of God leads you to repentance" (Romans 2:4) and "with love and kindness have I drawn thee" (Jeremiah 31:3, KJV).

Many of our Bible studies were held outside next to the driveway where our neighbors met their customers. When we had food, we always invited our neighbors and their customers to join us for meals. In the first few weeks, our neighbors threw illegal substances over the backyard fence that divided the properties to entice our men to use again. To the credit of our men and to the glory of God, our men threw the packages back over the fence. It was only God's mercy and grace. The GT Men had a genuine love for our neighbors (after all, they had been where they were just days, weeks, or months before) and prayed often for their salvation. Like the rest of us, our neighbors were filled with potential but needed direction.

Why were we so convinced that lives could be changed? Many of the rehab center (Potter's House) staff members were living testimonies of God's power because their lives, too, had been turned around. There was no greater example than Mike, our men's home director. Only a few years earlier, he had walked into Glad Tidings Church on Tennyson on a Sunday morning, accompanied by his wife and children. According to Mike and his wife, it was to be their last day together. His drug use was wrecking the family, so she was leaving to return to New York. Although he had been in the military and was a skilled X-ray technician, he was also a former distributor and now a crack addict. The day before they came to our service, he pushed beyond the limit and returned home completely consumed by crack cocaine. He convinced his wife to at least come to church with him before she left. His mother had told him that he needed to go to church.

Mike had heard of our church through a military colleague. When he and his family walked into the sanctuary, he was still high from the night before. The family sat in the back of our small church.

I finished preaching that morning and gave the altar call for people who wanted God to work in their lives. Mike wobbled down the aisle. I laid hands on him and began to pray, without knowing all that he was going through. Within moments, the Holy Spirit had slain him, and he was lying prostrate on the floor. After a short time, he rose from the floor and declared that his life was gloriously changed! His wife, however, wasn't convinced. She had heard this kind of story before. She told me, "Pastor, don't believe him. He's a liar. This is what he does. It is a scam; I know this man."

After pleading with her for almost an hour, I asked if she would give God a chance for three days. She responded, "Sir, he can't go straight for three days."

But through the power of Jesus Christ, Mike did go straight, and today, he has the testimony of a recovered addict. He became a very successful businessman and a noted ex-ray technician. It was Mike's vision and that of other men like him, and their relationships with men who struggle with addiction that drove the success of the Potter's House. This was heart change, life change, and a new legacy for the families of these men—all by the power of God.

By the way, our next-door neighbors moved out within a few weeks. We continued Bible studies in the driveways of the complex. We kept witnessing door to door, and we began to see a turnaround in the complex.

Later, I returned to the owner and said, "Sir, do you see the change taking place? It's remarkable, isn't it? We want to purchase the entire complex, all sixty-three units."

He was hesitant and told me, "Pastor, if I decide to sell, I'll let you know." A few months later, the call came. We had very little money but great faith. I was convinced by this point that you could buy property with no money down. God worked a miracle, and with the owner's cooperation, we purchased the entire complex.

We managed the project through our Community Development Corporation, but we never had the money to repair the units to our high standards. We discovered another, unexpected solution: many of our members began to move into the complex, and they brought light and hope. Once a year on Labor Day, the entire church worked on the property—GT was all in: painting, cleanup, landscaping, including rolling out grass and planting flowers. The church, on many occasions, invested thousands of dollars to keep the complex moving forward. The new name wasn't "Pink Palace II." Instead, the complex and the neighborhood embraced the new name, "Faith Manor."

In 2017, after fifteen years of ownership, the Glad Tidings CDC entered into a partnership with one of the largest nonprofit housing developers in the state of California. Their purchase and continued partnership have brought millions of dollars to complete the renovation of Faith Manor. Today, it's one of the most beautiful complexes in the city. Ultra-modern and regal, it will bring tears to your eyes. Now, residents are smiling and enjoying life in a way no one ever dreamed possible.

When God gives us a vision, and we have faith "the size of a grain of a mustard seed," He responds by expanding our faith, providing resources, and giving us enough tests to keep us humble and teach us important lessons. Ask God to open your eyes to see great things. By faith, set up your canvas. In his first letter to the Corinthians, Paul raises their eye level:

> But as it is written: "Eye has not seen, nor ear heard, Nor have entered into the heart of man the things which God has prepared for those who love Him."
>
> But God has revealed them to us through His Spirit. For the Spirit searches all things, yes, the deep things of God. For what man knows the things of a man except the spirit of the man which is in him? Even so no one knows the things of God except the Spirit of God. Now we have received, not the spirit of the world, but the Spirit who is from God, that we might know the things that have been freely given to us by God. —1 Corinthians 2:9-12

God has great things for you. Believe it. Walk in it. Enjoy it.

CONSIDER THIS:

1) Why do you think Nehemiah went on his long reconnaissance of Jerusalem at night instead of during the day? What did he avoid? What did he gain?

2) How do you respond to leaders who communicate a vision but don't seem to grasp the difficulties everyone faces?

3) What were some benefits of Nehemiah taking a few men with him on the night tour of the city?

4) Read Powhatan James's quote again, and paraphrase it here:

5) Do you agree or disagree with the idea that life is a series of increasingly difficult tests of our faith and endurance? Explain your answer.

6) What is God saying to you in this chapter? What is your vision for your family, your career, your church, and your community?

WORD ON THE STREET

LARRY MOODY

Former Mayor of East Palo Alto, California

I've been a member of Glad Tidings International for twenty-eight years. My wife and I got married at the church, and our four sons came to faith and were baptized there. We've had a front row seat to witness and participate in many of the events Bishop Macklin describes in this book. However, I want to describe evidence of the Bishop's impact that isn't in the book.

For ten years, I served as the Director of Local and Urban Ministries for Menlo Park Presbyterian Church. It was a bit of an odd fit for a Black Pentecostal to work on the staff of the largest Presbyterian (and mostly white) church in this part of the state. I hoped the staff team and the people of the Menlo Park church would see the value of both communities.

One day in 2004, I was in a staff meeting led by the gifted speaker, author, and leader, John Ortberg. He announced that he was cancelling our involvement in the church's annual five-day family camp. It was something our people looked forward to, but John felt it wasn't right for that year. One of us raised the issue that the church had already paid $80,000, and it was nonrefundable. We tried to debate with John to change his mind, but he was firm in his conviction. I raised my hand and said, "Why don't you give me a little time to talk to Bishop Macklin to see if he can pull something together, so the money isn't wasted."

John was sure it wasn't possible, but he told me, "I don't see how it can happen, but okay, you have four days."

I smiled and responded, "You don't know Bishop Macklin."

The next afternoon in a meeting with the Bishop, it all came together.

A few days later, more than three hundred people—pastors and their leadership teams—arrived at the camp. They represented African-American, Latino, and Pacific Island communities throughout the area, largely small, poor churches that couldn't have afforded the original cost of the event. They came because of the generous gift of Menlo Park Presbyterian and their desire to spend time with Bishop Macklin. The Bishop enlisted top speakers to come from all points of the nation to equip and inspire these leaders. When John realized what the event had become, he asked to speak on the first night at the opening session. He looked out at an audience that was very different from any he had seen at Menlo Park Presbyterian. He had a huge whiteboard behind the podium. His opening comment was, "How many churches are here tonight?"

People looked around to see who from their churches was raising a hand. Everyone began to calculate the number, but John turned and wrote a big "1." He told the three hundred leaders, "There's one church here. Just one. Pastor Macklin convened all of us—no matter our race, color, or background—to be one church together."

The rest of the event went to the next level of spiritual power, excellence, and authenticity. People were honest about their struggles, and the speakers gave rich, strong, practical input on a range of topics to help them lead more effectively. John invited Dallas Willard, the author of Divine Conspiracy, to speak. He sat in the middle of everyone and talked like a beloved uncle about how our relationships with each other shape every aspect of our lives, including our love for God and how we lead the people God has put in our care. John came back to the camp on the second day because he was so thirsty for the love and support he felt from the participants, and he said he wanted to learn how to lead from Bishop Macklin.

The Bishop created an environment where leaders felt valued and received tools, training, and resources to help them excel still more in their calling, but the connections didn't end when the cars left the camp on the last day. Lasting friendships were developed. For instance, the pastors from our city began a network called A Fellowship of Faith to pray for each other, share our hearts, and encourage each other.

When I walked through the doors of Glad Tidings twenty-eight years ago, I needed Jesus to redeem me. Like the prodigal in the parable, I was climbing out of the pigpen and finding my way home. Under Bishop Macklin's love and leadership, I've been saved, God has turned my life around, and I've seen Him at work through that humble, kind, and fierce advocate for "the least of these." It has been, and continues to be, a high honor and a great privilege to know him.

CHAPTER 7

FIGHTING ABOVE YOUR WEIGHT CLASS

Nehemiah Confronted People No One Else Was Willing to Confront

You've heard the saying, "No good deed goes unpunished." We might also conclude, "No great vision goes unopposed." It happens. It always happens. And it happened to Nehemiah. In fact, it happened at the beginning and throughout the reconstruction project. Immediately after the inspection and the call for the people to join the effort, we see the first glimpse of opposition:

> *But when Sanballat the Horonite, Tobiah the Ammonite official, and Geshem the Arab heard of it, they laughed at us and despised us, and said, "What is this thing that you are doing? Will you rebel against the king?"* —Nehemiah 2:19

Their ridicule took two different forms: they laughed with contempt, and they accused Nehemiah of treason. Rebelling against the king was a capital offense, deserving execution. That's a far more serious charge than "You don't know what you're doing!"

Notice that they asked pointed questions. That's often the best way to accuse someone while appearing to be dispassionate. Look at their questions again. They were asking:

» Who is this who has come to seek the welfare of the pitiful Jews?

» Who has the gall to defy the king?

» Who has the nerve to think these walls can be rebuilt?

» Who is foolish enough to try to change the culture of the city?

Imagine the scene: Nehemiah had just enlisted the cooperation of the demoralized people of the city. Finally, they had hope. Finally, they had a leader. Finally, things were going to be different! Their newfound courage was real but probably fragile. The two accusers assumed a scathing word would stop them cold, but Nehemiah defended himself and the people who had rallied to the cause: "So I answered them, and said to them, 'The God of heaven Himself will prosper us; therefore we His servants will arise and build, but you have no heritage or right or memorial in Jerusalem'" (v. 20).

Take that, Sanballat and Tobiah! Nehemiah was saying (as much to his people as to the two opponents), "God called me here, and God called His people to join me!"

We also need to understand that the only person who needed an introduction in this encounter was Nehemiah. The people of the city had lived under the contempt of Sanballat and Tobiah for a long time. They'd seen the two men glare at them, and they'd heard them speak to them (and about them) with derision. In this pivotal moment, they could have been overwhelmed by a toxic deluge of memories of being dominated by the two opponents. It took great courage for Nehemiah to stand up to Sanballat and Tobiah, but it took just as much (and maybe more) courage for the people to stand by Nehemiah's side.

In the face of the Pharisees' opposition, Jesus warned the disciples, "Behold, I send you out as sheep in the midst of wolves. Therefore be as wise as serpents and as harmless as doves" (Matthew 10:16). That's exactly what Nehemiah was doing: he expected opposition, so he wasn't flustered when it came.

Are there people in your family who don't want you to be whole and healthy? When you were weak and vulnerable, you were more easily manipulated. When you walk with Jesus and learn to speak the truth in love, at least some of the people who used to control you through their anger, tears, abuse, or abandonment won't like it one bit. They prefer you to remain under their thumbs! In the same way, when a church begins to trust God to transform their surrounding community, opposition is guaranteed. It may come from obvious places like haters on the streets or others who feel threatened, but it may also come from bureaucrats or community leaders who profit from the status quo. They may promise change in their campaigns for election and reelection, but when they're in office, they may resist change even as they smile at you and assure you they're on your side. In our relationships with them, we need to follow Jesus' advice: Be shrewd—not naïve. And be self-controlled—not yelling in defiance.

In a remarkable account in Mark's Gospel (Mark 5:1-20), Jesus and His disciples crossed over the Sea of Galilee to the area inhabited by the Gadarenes. When Jesus stepped out of the boat, a man possessed by demons appeared. He had been living among the dead in the tombs. He was an outcast's outcast—far from God and despised by people. They feared him because his supernatural strength enabled him to break chains and shackles. They also heard him. Day and night he screamed as he gashed himself with sharp rocks. In one of the most poignant and tender scenes in the Gospels, the man ran toward Jesus (What were the disciples thinking at that moment?), fell at His feet, and worshiped Him. A demonic voice called out from inside him, "What have I to do with You, Jesus, Son of the Most High God? I implore You by God that You do not torment me."

Jesus asked the demon to identify himself. It responded, "My name is Legion; for we are many."

The demons begged Jesus to cast them into a herd of pigs, and when He did, the pigs ran into the sea and drowned. The people of the city who had watched it all didn't shout, "Hallelujah! God has done great things today!" No, when they saw the man "sitting and clothed and in his right mind," they begged Jesus to leave their area.

The man understandably wanted to go with Jesus, the one whose love and power had so radically transformed his existence, but Jesus sent him on a missionary journey to his friends and family: "Go home to your friends, and tell them what great things the Lord has done for you, and how He has had compassion on you."

And he did just that: "And he departed and began to proclaim in Decapolis all that Jesus had done for him, and all marveled." The demoniac, now delivered, looked at himself on the canvas of tomorrow that Jesus had given him, and off he went.

When God uses you to do great things for Him, some will applaud, others will jeer, and still others will run away because miracles make them feel uncomfortable. I've seen this range of responses happen in families when someone has come to Christ and seen genuine life change, and I've seen it in our community as neighbors and city officials have witnessed God's work in and through our church.

FIGHTING ABOVE YOUR WEIGHT CLASS

Round 1

The boxer Sugar Ray Leonard had legendary toughness, and he often agreed to fight men who were bigger and stronger . . . and he usually won the bouts. He commented that our willingness to be challenged is the mark of our character: "It's what you take on that defines you." At Glad Tidings, we had to take on some giants and fight above our weight class more than once.

In Hayward in 1978, an old gas station stood on the corner of Tennyson Road and Tyrrell Avenue, one short block from the church that God would give us. While it would be three years before we moved into the neighborhood, I often drove through the area I had claimed by faith. I believed the corner was strategic for the future of a revitalized community, and I began calling the corner "The Glad Tidings Gateway."

I was sure God would give us the corner to the major intersection into the neighborhood, but I had no idea how to make it happen. I began to speak what I could only see in the Spirit, first to myself and then to a few others. I spoke what I had envisioned until I could see more clearly what I had spoken. With God as our trusted partner, we had begun the long, audacious, and tedious task of transforming a forgotten and downtrodden community. The 62-unit apartment building had been purchased, now named Faith Manor, along with the renovated 8-plex, GT Arms. Fifteen families had purchased Spring Court condos. This corner was the gateway and set the atmosphere for the rest of the community—but at the time, it was a broken gate, and it created a bleak atmosphere.

Former gas station.

From the time I first drove past the corner, the gas station was long gone, and the site had been purchased by a popular food chain. However, their proposed development had not begun, and I soon discovered why. We approached the company about purchasing the site. They quickly agreed to sell, and we agreed on a price of a little more than $200,000. However, there was one catch: the agreement was based on a clean soils report. We discovered that the site was originally owned by Chevron Oil, which had only completed a partial cleanup when they abandoned the gas station. Our option to purchase required a complete cleanup.

The property owner made no moves to have it cleaned up, but we wanted that corner, so we moved up to another weight division to face a powerful foe, one of America's Fortune 500 companies. We had no money to fight, no attorney, and no corporate partners to help us. But as Paul would say when he was in the Roman prison, God sent an angel and strengthened him (Acts 27:23). There was no question that we needed God's strength!

Hugh is a good friend who was in charge of environmental concerns in the city. I explained that Chevron Oil had left the corner without properly cleaning it. The corner was an eyesore, and the weeds, rocks, and debris had become a playground for kids in the neighborhood. I asked Hugh if we could force Chevron Oil to clean it up. He said it was a long shot, but he was willing to set up a meeting. To our surprise, Chevron sent two high-ranking representatives to meet us in the city's conference room—David and Goliath were scheduled to face off at 9:00 a.m.! They were invited in, but I waited until they were seated before I entered the room. I didn't have a written script; instead, I trusted God for the words to say. When I walked in, Hugh introduced me: "Gentlemen, this is Rev. Macklin." Then he introduced them: "Rev. Macklin, these men are from Chevron Oil." They stared at me, and I stared back at them. You could cut the tension with a knife.

I spoke first: "Gentlemen, your company left a gas station site in our neighborhood without cleaning it up, and our children are now playing in this polluted area. I want to know what you're going to do about the problem."

One of the men from Chevron responded in very detailed terms, but in effect, he told us that they were using "a natural method," and the pollutants would decompose over time. I asked, "Over time? Is this the way you'd clean up sites like this in upscale neighborhoods, like Walnut Creek, Concord, or Pleasanton? I know the answer. You would never leave an abandoned gas station in other neighborhoods, but somehow you feel justified doing it in ours. I think not!"

I stood up and looked over my glasses toward Hugh and said, "I told you they wouldn't understand, but they will. They'll see me again, but they won't like it. I've got this!" I left the conference room and closed the door without saying goodbye or shaking hands.

As I was walking away, I could hear Hugh warning them, "You don't know Rev. Macklin. You've made a big mistake." A few seconds later, the door re-opened, and a voice called after me, "Come back, Reverend. We'll clean it up."

Soon, equipment was brought to the corner property, a fence was installed, and the work was begun. The cleanup process took more than a year and cost tens of thousands of dollars. I didn't know how much the work would cost, and frankly, I didn't care. I only knew that they wouldn't treat other neighborhoods in the same way.

Finally, the work was complete, and it was time for us to exercise our option to purchase the property. As I was circling the neighborhood, I saw an unusual—and alarming—sight: a man was using a weed eater on the lot. I pulled in and asked, "Hey, man, what are you doing?" He informed me that his aunt had just purchased the land, and they were preparing to build a nail salon and another business on the site.

I responded sharply, "What are you talking about? This land belongs to the church, and it's not for sale!"

He shot back, "My aunt already bought this site and has the papers to prove it!"

I told him, "Call her now! Get her on the phone."

After more than a year, our option had run out, but I had been sure the restaurant chain would honor our contract. I was wrong. As soon as the agreement expired, they found a buyer willing to pay a higher price for a clean site, and they sold it out from under us.

I had no time for lawyers, city officials, or corporate representatives. This was no time for a letter-writing campaign or a social media blitz. I needed divine intervention, and I needed it now! The man called his aunt and handed me his phone. Even though she had an accent, I could understand her clearly. I began, "I don't know who you are, but you can't buy this property. It belongs to God!"

She answered back, "You are a crazy man! I have the title deed, and this is my property. I just bought it."

I responded, "I don't know who sold this to you, but this property belongs to God, and you can't buy it!" I quickly understood that we both had been double-crossed. I said, "Lady, this is God's property, and you don't want it. Whatever you paid for it, meet me on this corner tomorrow at noon, and I'll give you what you paid plus $20,000."

She responded, "I will do no such thing."

I shouted back, "Yes, you will!" and hung up the phone. I got in my car and drove away.

The next day at noon, a dear lady showed up on the corner. She was shaking, with papers in hand, and as I walked near, she shouted, "Take it! Take it!" I spoke to her calmly and assured her it was the right thing to do.

You can't seize what you can't see. Your crisis isn't the size of your problem; it's the size of your vision. Can you see what God wants to show you? Abraham, lift your eyes and see. The grass may not be well-watered, but look! The grass may not be green and inviting, but look! Go ahead, tell me what you see. Look beyond what you see. For us, the challenge at hand wasn't simply to clean up an abandoned lot; it was to provide a safe environment for the people in our neighborhood. That's why I was so determined to buy the corner lot.

The process of purchasing the corner took a month or so, but finally, it was done. The once-abandoned, neglected, and dangerous site had been cleaned. I have no idea how many children had been poisoned by playing on that site, but now it was over. It was safe and secure in our hands . . . in God's hands.

Others may have seen this corner as a gateway to criminal activity, but I had seen it as a gateway to a changing neighborhood. Only days after we completed the purchase, we began landscaping and converting it into additional parking for the campus and our new church sanctuary, but it was so much more than that. As thousands passed this corner every day, this once-blighted junction became a sign of hope for a community worth saving. For corporate America, it was a signal that doing what's right for a community is always the right thing to do. And to the church, the message once again was, "Greater is He who is in you than he who is in the world"—even corporate America! Today, flags fly on this corner, the gateway to our neighborhood. Yes, the American flag and the California flag, but more importantly, the Glad Tidings flag waves there too, indicating that our God reigns. This corner is a sign of a transformed community. It points beyond itself to people who live, work, and worship here. It's a gateway to a renovated community, and it's an open door to families who feel forgotten by a system they feel has abandoned them.

On the canvas of tomorrow, the church was ushering in a new way for residents to look at their community. More importantly, it ushered in a new way for residents to look at themselves.

Round 2

The story of Nehemiah is one of a remarkable leader and dedicated followers. He enlisted everyone who was willing to work, organized them, assigned them, provided resources for them, and encouraged them to labor alongside their families at the places in the wall that would protect their homes. Nehemiah was a master at motivating people!

The work progressed at an amazing pace, which didn't exactly change the mood of the antagonists. They redoubled their attacks. This was Round 2:

> But it so happened, when Sanballat heard that we were rebuilding the wall, that he was furious and very indignant, and mocked the Jews. And he spoke before his brethren and the army of Samaria, and said, "What are these feeble Jews doing? Will they fortify themselves? Will they offer sacrifices? Will they complete it in a day? Will they revive the stones from the heaps of rubbish—stones that are burned?"
>
> Now Tobiah the Ammonite was beside him, and he said, "Whatever they build, if even a fox goes up on it, he will break down their stone wall." —Nehemiah 4:1-3

For these two, cold contempt had given way to fury and rage! Sanballat may have thought his initial scorn would intimidate Nehemiah and the people, but now he realized he needed bigger guns. He enlisted the help of an army, using the same kind of ridicule against the Jews that he had used before. And Tobiah, not to be ignored, insisted that the wall they were building wouldn't even hold up if a little fox walked on it. (Which begs the question: If it was that flimsy, why were these two guys so upset? The answer is obvious: They knew better. They were sure this was going to be a turning point in the city, one that would leave them out of power.)

Again, Nehemiah didn't depend on his exemplary leadership skills or the strong backs of the builders. He voiced his dependence on God, and he trusted Him to bring justice for the accusers:

> Hear, O our God, for we are despised; turn their reproach on their own heads, and give them as plunder to a land of captivity! Do not cover their iniquity, and do not let their sin be blotted out from before You; for they have provoked You to anger before the builders. —vv. 4-5

For the first fifteen years of my life, I grew up at Macedonia Church of God in Christ at 66 N. Claremont Street, San Mateo, California. On the wall in the small sanctuary was a sign. It had always been there, and now I know why. It read:

> *So built we the wall; and all the wall was joined together unto the half thereof: for the people had a mind to. —vv. 4-6*

At Glad Tidings, we had a Round 2 of our own: Save Mart (Frys) grocery store was a major chain with a successful store in South Hayward on Tennyson Road. For many years, it provided the neighborhood with the full line of products. To the surprise of many, the store suddenly announced it was closing. Not only was it closing, but it was moving across the freeway and opening as a big-box grocery store.

Closing the store meant the neighborhood would become a food desert. There would be no grocery store that could supply food for families that lived in that part of South Hayward. It was a tragedy in the making. It wasn't long before I realized that we had to do something, and we had to do something quickly.

With the help of our city councilman, Olden Henson, we began to investigate our options. After a few days, we discovered that our best chance was to step into the ring with the executives of Save Mart. We made an appointment and drove to see the chairman of the board in Modesto, California, nearly one hundred miles away. We challenged the board chairman, insisting that he couldn't close the store in our neighborhood because it would bring such hardships to the people. We also explained that the company had made a lot of money from us over the years, so we felt they had a responsibility to keep the store open. The new store, on the other side of the freeway, would require our people to walk across the bridge over the freeway in heavy traffic. Some residents simply weren't able to haul bags of groceries back over the bridge to their homes. This, we explained, was going to create insurmountable problems for many of them.

We appealed to the city for their help to block Save Mart's plan or partner with us to discover an alternative. The local newspaper carried the story of a minister who fights for a grocery store in the neighborhood. Ours, however, was more than just a typical battle. People's lives were at stake, and their quality of living was at stake.

It was time to step into the ring. I believed deeply that the church had to be at the forefront of fighting for the neighborhood. After intense negotiations and assistance from the city, we failed in our efforts to convince Save Mart executives to keep their store in South Hayward.

I didn't want to burn all the bridges with Save Mart, so we continued to work with them in hopes of locating another grocery store willing to locate in our community. Save Mart agreed to sell their store location to another grocer if we could identify a viable company. They even offered to leave some of the appliances and other equipment, if that would be helpful. The city agreed to work with us to overcome many of the challenges in attracting a new business. So now, the search was on. We had an opportunity, but the window was closing fast.

I explained the challenge to our congregation. At first, I began to investigate the possibility of a Black-owned grocery store. After some time, I discovered that wasn't a realistic possibility. Then, God gave us an unexpected open door. One of our members, Anita, a graduate of Cal State Hayward, worked as a social worker in San Mateo County. She mentioned to a co-worker that her pastor was fighting to save the neighborhood grocery store, and she told him about the possibility of bringing a new grocery store to our neighborhood to keep it from becoming a food desert. To her surprise, her co-worker said, "My husband owns three grocery stores, but they're on the Peninsula. I could have him talk with your pastor and see if there's a possibility of opening a store in Hayward." Sure enough, her husband called. After lengthy conversations and touring the property, we determined that this could be a possibility.

Within a few short months, Chavez Supermarket opened a new, ultra-modern store in the location where Save Mart had been. New life was infused into our community. It's a Mexican American supermarket, but it caters to a diverse population. The food is great, the meat is fresh, and the produce is always delicious. A new business had been born on Tennyson, just a few doors from the church. Today, the store has expanded, taking over adjacent properties. It's a thriving business with a bakery and a delicatessen. In addition to that location, Chavez Market has opened a new store on Mission Boulevard, near downtown.

Chavez Supermarket is thriving because the church refused to allow a food desert in the neighborhood. We fought hard. We were bloodied in the battle, but we came out on top. All glory to God!

Round 3

You have to give Sanballat and Tobiah credit. They were as tenacious in opposition as Nehemiah and the people were tenacious in their faith to keep building. When the wall was half-finished, the two antagonists enlisted three other adversaries—the Arabs, the Ammonites, and the Ashdodites—to join their conspiracy against God's people.

Nehemiah heard rumors of dissension from every corner:

> *The strength of the laborers is failing, and there is so much rubbish that we are not able to build the wall." And our adversaries said, "They will neither know nor see anything, till we come into their midst and kill them and cause the work to cease." So it was, when the Jews who dwelt near them came, that they told us ten times, "From whatever place you turn, they will be upon us." —Nehemiah 4:10-12*

Did Nehemiah collapse mentally and emotionally? Were the threats enough to stop the enterprise? No way! He again rose to the challenge, calling out the best in them and giving them the greatest incentive to keep working:

> *Therefore I positioned men behind the lower parts of the wall, at the openings; and I set the people according to their families, with their swords, their spears, and their bows. And I looked, and arose and said to the nobles, to the leaders, and to the rest of the people, "Do not be afraid of them. Remember the Lord, great and awesome, and fight for your brethren, your sons, your daughters, your wives, and your houses." —vv. 13-14*

To meet the threat, Nehemiah ordered half of the workers to continue building while the other half stood guard, and even those who kept working had a weapon, so they'd be ready if an attack came. They stayed on the wall day and night. And they kept building.

Fear isn't always a mirage. Sometimes it's the only realistic reaction. In 2010, a young man ran into New Gethsemane Church in Richmond, California, to kill a rival gang member. Instead, he killed the man's two younger brothers as they were running away and turning in front of the altar. The congregation was understandably traumatized by the event, and the pastor asked me to come to minister to his congregation. I went the very next day to speak to the people who had been so deeply affected by this senseless violence.

When I arrived, the church was packed with people who had been in the service when the gunman ran in, but also present were banks of television cameras and rows of reporters from local newspapers, radio stations, and television networks. When I stood up to speak, I told them, "Ladies and gentlemen, my name is Bishop Jerry Macklin. This church is one of those for whom I'm responsible. I came today to take responsibility for what happened. This is my fault. What happened in your church yesterday is my fault. I want to apologize."

The crowd gasped. That's not the message they had expected to hear. I continued, "If I had done a better job of equipping this church to reach young people with the love and life-changing power of the gospel of Jesus Christ, the gunman may have been in church worshiping yesterday instead of shooting. Because I'm taking responsibility, let me say what I think we need to do to address the crisis of violence in this community. Next Saturday morning, I invite all the men of this city to meet me here. We're going to knock on ten thousand doors and give away ten thousand Bibles."

At that moment, a lady in the back of the church stood up and yelled, "Excuse me, sir, but you sound like a male chauvinist! How can you have the event for men only?"

I replied, "Ma'am, I may be a chauvinist, but I don't think I am. This is the way I was raised. Our family moved into San Mateo when I was just a boy. We were the first Black family to integrate the Shoreview neighborhood. My brother and I were prepared to fight our way home from school every day. People threw eggs at our house and put dead animals on our porch. At night, when we heard a noise outside, my father was equipped with the gift of the Holy Spirit and the gift of a twelve gauge shotgun. Before he stepped out the door, he always told my mother, 'Helen, stay inside and keep the door closed. Make sure the children stay in bed. I'll be back.' We might have

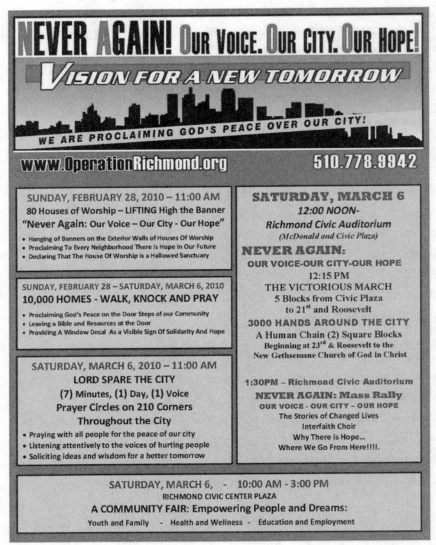

heard him say or do something, or it might have been completely quiet, but he always came back." I then explained, "Ma'am, my father never told my mother to go outside and protect the house and the family. He believed that was his role. My father loved and protected his family. In the same way, I can't imagine telling you to go out on the streets to confront the gangs. The gangs are predominately young men, and the men of the city need to address the problem. After all, they are our sons."

After the meeting, I had a real problem: Where was I going to come up with ten thousand Bibles? I called my friend, Ted Squires, the vice president of Thomas Nelson

Publishers in Nashville, and I asked him to send the Bibles to me. I'm not sure where he found them, but on Friday, a truck and trailer backed up to the church in Richmond and unloaded the ten thousand Bibles from the American Bible Society.

The next morning at 11:00, men and women from forty or fifty churches went to designated street corners to pray before we began our event. Then, 2,300 people showed up at the church. We gave them stacks of Bibles, gave them directions to different neighborhoods, and sent them out two by two. We put signs all over the city that read, "Never Again!" Our Glad Tidings men brought an enormous barbeque pit and fed people all day.

One man spoke for many when he saw the outpouring of love: "Richmond will be a better place."

The pastor of New Gethsemane, Pastor Archie Levias, proclaimed, "Never again. Never again will there be violence in our churches. Never again."

When I spoke, I addressed the sense of helplessness and despair: "You know what? If we don't stand up now, when are we going to stand up?"

A news reporter on the scene that day wrote, "To make it clear that the wrong doing will stop, especially around New Gethsemane Church, hundreds clasped hands and formed a prayer circle. Their arms stretched around the entire church and around the entire square block. It even caused people on the street to stop and take notice."[11]

While the event was happening, I asked someone to take me to meet with the chief drug lord of the city. The person was stunned, "Bishop, you can't do that! It's not safe."

I convinced him that I wanted to go. Someone had the right connections, and not long after that, I was ushered into an alley in the Iron Triangle where I walked alone. When we got close enough, both of us stopped and sized each other up. We stood and talked for about thirty minutes. I told him, "We can't have gang members going into churches shooting people."

---

11 "Hundreds gather to stand up against crime in Richmond," *ABC7 CHICAGO*, 6 Mar. 2010, https://abc7chicago.com/archive/7316105/.

He nodded, "I know, Reverend. That's not going to happen again. I guarantee it."

I didn't ask how he was going to follow through on his promise, but I ended our meeting by saying, "Thank you. I want you to know that I love you, and I believe God has something better for you." He was extremely respectful and polite, and I was the same. I prayed for him, and I turned and walked away.

A few weeks later, I was honored by the Richmond city council for the effectiveness of the Never Again campaign. One city official remarked that crime began dropping significantly following the Saturday event. The churches and faith community of Richmond had stood together, and change had come. The Richmond city council recognized the work of the ministry with an official resolution in the city council meeting of March 16, 2010: "Operation Richmond was a direct response to the February 14 shooting at the New Gethsemane Church in Richmond." The resolution went on to read, "Operation Richmond coordinated thousands of households to walk their blocks and pray, to profess peace for our community." The resolution closed with the council commending and honoring the collective efforts of Operation Richmond for standing up against violence and promoting peace, unity, and harmony in our communities.

ONE BLOOD

In Minneapolis, Minnesota, George Floyd Jr., a Black American, was murdered in the custody of police on May 20, 2020. A short time later a very sincere pastor called, who later would become a dear friend, ask me to participate in a community effort to encourage peace in our cities. The request was to join other pastors at one of the largest churches in the Bay Area to record short videos. The compilation was to be called, "You Are My Neighbor" the Good Samaritan Story. The pastor respectfully asked, "can you join with us by coming to record your video?" I responded, "I'm not coming."

He was surprised and asked, "Why not? Your presence is important to this effort." I told him, "Thank you, but I'm not coming." He asked again why I did not want to participate. So, I explained, "you have 15 or 20 pastors driving to a church to record videos highlighting how we are neighbors. Many of the pastors you have invited have never stopped in my neighborhood to speak or say hello. Now they are asked to drive past our neighborhood to record the Samaritan story. I ask, does that sound like a neighbor to you?"

I went on, "You can't act like my neighbor on television or YouTube and not have the courtesy to drop by and get to know me." I continued, "If you want to get together to talk about the issues of policing and injustice, I'd be happy to have you. Tomorrow at 10:00 in the morning, I'll be on a Zoom call with anyone who wants to explore the issues we face."

The following day almost 15 pastors (many who have become friends) were on the call. We had a frank and productive conversation. After one year, we still meet on Wednesday mornings to dialogue concerning what it means to be a neighbor in a fractured, hate-filled society. We explore the importance of speaking the truth in love, and truth to power, pushing past emotional and spiritual exhaustion to engage people who disagree with us, and reaching out to people who aren't like us—and in fact, don't like us. The morning dialogue evolved into what has become known as "the One Blood Group." We've asked God to give us a better understanding of what it means to love our neighbors as ourselves. Today, political polarization has created a deep division in the nation and among Christians. Can't we value God's kingdom more than political power? Can't we follow the One who is the only source of love, life, and justice instead of bickering with each other to score political points? As we began, I remember asking, "what does it means when a Black American utters the words, I'm tired?"

I sometimes ask aloud but always ponder in my heart: *How can we sit with each other on a pew in worship and refuse to stand with each other when we witness injustice?* In Jesus' parable of the Good Samaritan, the worshippers walked past a man, robbed, beaten, and left for dead. They were *on their way* to church, but they failed at *being* the church in the moment. The poignant point in the story is that a hated Samaritan, an outcast despised by the Jews, was the one who showed overflowing compassion to the Jew who lay broken and bleeding in the street. May I ask in this story: Who are you? Who am I? Who are we?

Our One Blood Group endeavors to tear down walls of prejudice and suspicion. We're committed to building walls of understanding and protection. Conversations like these are often uncomfortable, but encourage us to paint on the canvas of a better, brighter, more just tomorrow.

CONSIDER THIS:

1) Do you think Nehemiah expected opposition from the moment he announced the project to rebuild the city walls? Why or why not?

2) How have you seen it to be true that some people (in your family, your friendships, and your community) want you to be weak and vulnerable, and they don't like it when you're becoming strong and healthy?

3) Describe Nehemiah's response to confrontation at the beginning and as the wall was being built.

4) The common ways people respond to stress and opposition include fleeing, fighting, and freezing. What is your default mode when you feel threatened? What's the default mode of those close to you? How does it help to identify these patterns?

5) Should Christians build protective walls around themselves, their families, their churches, and their neighborhoods? Explain your answer.

6) What is God saying to you in this chapter? What walls do you need to build?

WORD ON THE STREET

SHERYL BOYKINS

Former Police Lieutenant, Hayward, California

South Hayward was known for drugs, gangs, and all kinds of criminal activity, and the neighborhood specifically around Bishop Macklin's church was the worst. His vision for cleaning up and renovating the community involved community policing, which I was assigned to lead.

One day he called and asked me to visit with him. When we met, he told me he was concerned that a local gang called "the D-boys" had started congregating on a corner at Forselles Street near the church. The gang had a reputation that was well-deserved, and the Bishop told me that his people had expressed their fear of walking past the gang on the way to church. We decided to walk the streets together to show our solidarity. As we walked on the sidewalk on Forselles, both of us noticed that a car approaching us was slowing down. That was during the time when drive-by shootings were fairly common, so we were rightly afraid of what might happen. The Bishop's life had been threatened before, and I was wearing my uniform, which some considered a prime target. As the car got closer, the rear window started to come down. I could feel my heart beat under my Kevlar vest. As the car got next to us, I imagined a gun sticking out of the window, but instead, a young man leaned out and yelled, "Yo, Bishop! Is everything okay?" I felt immediate and overwhelming relief, and from the look on his face, Bishop Macklin did too. The man who yelled to him was a gangbanger, but the Bishop had earned his respect. It wasn't a drive-by shooting; it was a drive-by affirmation of Bishop Macklin's love and leadership.

I knew the members of the D-boys, and I made sure they knew me. When they were hanging out too near the church, I asked one of their leaders, "Could you just move it up the street a couple of blocks away from the church? The kids are ready to come home from school, and mothers are pushing strollers and walking toddlers. We don't need you to intimidate them, so please, move on."

He smiled and said, "Okay, Boykins, but you owe me." He turned to walk up the street, and the rest followed him.

About two weeks later, that young man was shot. I went to see him in the hospital, and he asked me to take care of his baby mama and child, so they wouldn't be kicked out of their Section 8 apartment. I did, and when he got out of the hospital, he didn't forget what I'd done for him and his family. He often stopped by to check up on me to see how I was doing. This relationship is an example of how community policing can work to build trust and respect among people who previously looked on each other with suspicion. This kind of police work connects us more closely to the law-abiding citizens, and it builds relationships with the knuckleheads too.

No matter what was going on in the neighborhood, Bishop Macklin was right in the middle of it to care for those involved. In an apartment building near the church, a deranged grandmother stabbed her grandchildren to death. Everyone in the area knew and loved the kids, so it was traumatic for a lot of people. The Bishop stepped in to provide his presence and comfort, and he had the church provide a meal for everyone in the complex, so they could decompress, talk about the incident, and begin the process of grieving and healing. He invited those of us in law enforcement to come, so we could connect with the people who were devastated by the tragic event.

I worked that neighborhood for about ten years. I had opportunities to be trans-ferred to posts that had fewer calls and a less dense population, but I chose to stay in that part of South Hayward. I wanted to stay because Bishop Macklin created a culture where his people saw the police as an asset, not an adversary, and they were glad to cooperate with us.

CHAPTER 8

DOING ALL TO STAND

Nehemiah Stood Against Powers that Intimidated Others

People who oppose us are usually easy to identify. As a counselor observed, they "get big": glaring, yelling, accusing, leaning toward us in a menacing way. But some are more subtle and sly. They stab us in the back with a smile on their faces.

Our opponents usually have names and faces, but we also face a completely different category of threats: systems and mindsets. A system may be unspoken but very real ingrained cultural injustice—prejudice at least, if not racism. Housing, employment, and education are weighted toward certain segments of our society, but other groups are given less attention and fewer resources—and the difference is deeply embedded in government policies, banking, and prevailing attitudes. We can shrug and say, "That's the way it's been, that's the way it is, and that's the way it'll always be," or we can shout, "Enough!" And with courage, we can do something about it. We can seek the heart of God for vision and wisdom, and with brush in hand, begin painting on the canvas of a new tomorrow.

When we came to South Hayward, we stepped into a tilted power structure and negative expectations that had crippled the community. You might think that nobody benefits from this kind of system, but in any culture, certain people thrive on the hardships of others. They feel powerful when others are kept weak. They can play the role of heroes by merely showing they understand the situation while blaming someone else for the problem.

Nehemiah had to stand against the powerfully ingrained negative self-concept of the people of Jerusalem: their belief that they deserved their desperate condition, and there was nothing they could do to change it. After all, their parents and grandparents had rebelled against God, worshiped idols, and trusted in foreign countries for protection instead of trusting in the Lord. They had been crushed by the Assyrians and then the Babylonians. Now the Persians were the supreme power, and they were just as ruthless as the rest. For decades, God's people had been beaten down, starved, enslaved, and seemingly abandoned by God . . . but wasn't this exactly what they deserved? That was their conclusion.

Nehemiah was under no illusions that the people he was going to enlist in the construction project were skilled and eager. When he shared his vision of a new tomorrow, Nehemiah said, "You see the distress that we are in, how Jerusalem lies waste, and her gates are burned with fire. Come and let us build the wall of Jerusalem, that we may no longer be a reproach" (Nehemiah 2:17). They had lived in the ruins of the city so long that their lives resembled some of the apocalyptic movies about the end of time. Imagine trying to scratch out a living among the broken rocks and burned gates. Imagine your children crying from hunger, and imagine your spouse blaming you for not doing more.

The mindset of the people in Jerusalem was "learned helplessness," which, according to Psychology Today, "occurs when an individual continuously faces a negative, uncontrollable situation and stops trying to change their circumstances, even when they have the ability to do so."[12] Over time, their vision of the future becomes myopic, their hopes are nonexistent, and their energy level is negligible. We see it in the lives of addicts who have given up on ever getting clean and sober. We see it in the lives of spouses who have lived in despair so long that they have no hope of real change in their marriages. We see it in the lives of communities where generations of poverty have created an ingrained, pervasive discouragement. People who believe this about

12 "Learned Helplessness," *Psychology Today*, Sussex Publishers, www.psychologytoday.com/us/basics/learned-helplessness.

themselves have concluded they haven't just failed; they believe they're branded as failures. They've concluded that everything is out of their control, and whatever they try won't work anyway, so what's the use?

Into this quagmire of doom, stepped a man whose God-inspired vision for the future overcame a hopeless mindset. Nehemiah continually pointed people to God and reminded them of his love and power. He didn't give simple solutions to complex problems. Instead, he spoke the unvarnished truth about their condition, injected a new sense of hope, organized them, so they could see real progress, and led them through the internal and external attacks they suffered.

That's what it takes for a husband, a wife, a parent, a business leader, or a church leader to turn the people they lead from the pit to the pinnacle. In the process, we confront systems of banking that exclude people others don't want in their neighborhoods, we offer tangible instruction, so people can learn skills to escape the cycle of poverty, we fight city hall when our community is being ignored, and we speak up for the oppressed, whoever they are.

FLINT

In the summer of 2012, city officials in Flint, Michigan, looked for ways to save money on water provided to its citizens. After studying the options, the city chose to build a pipeline to the Karegnondi Water Authority to save a projected $200 million over the subsequent twenty-five years. Before the pipeline could be completed, they needed another source of water, so they used the Flint River.

The city released a statement acknowledging community concerns about the quality of the water, but officials assured residents the water was safe. Immediately, some residents complained about the smell and color of the water, and E. coli bacteria was found in samples, prompting advisories for people to boil water. A General Motors plant in the city stopped using water because engineers found it could result in corrosion of their equipment.

The following February, according to an NPR article written by Merrit Kennedy, a test of water quality revealed "high lead content in the water of a Flint resident's home."[13] Two months later, a child in the home was diagnosed with lead poisoning, almost three times the level when lead is considered hazardous waste. By July, however, officials insisted, "Anyone who is concerned about lead in the drinking water in Flint can relax."[14] Two months later, a study showed that the percentage of children with elevated blood lead levels had doubled since the switch to the Flint River.

On September 25, the city issued an advisory about the water, but the state governor's chief of staff lamented "that some in Flint are taking the very sensitive issue of children's exposure to lead and trying to turn it into a political football claiming the departments are underestimating the impacts on the population and particularly trying to shift responsibility to the state."[15] Still, a few weeks later, Flint switched its water supply back to the Great Lakes Water Authority, which, residents were assured, was completely safe.

But it wasn't. In December, the new mayor of Flint declared a state of emergency. Soon, state regulation officials resigned over the controversy, and the Environmental Protection Agency issued an emergency order about the crisis. In February, Michigan Governor Snyder testified before the US House Committee on Oversight and Government Reform, saying, "Let me be blunt. This was a failure of government at all levels. Local, state, and federal officials—we all failed the families of Flint." Almost a year after the debacle began, Flint's water was still unsafe, and criminal charges were filed against three officials. Subsequent lawsuits were filed against two companies that were accused of negligence and public nuisance, and then six other state employees were charged with misconduct, conspiracy, and willful neglect of duty.[16] To conclude that the crisis in Flint was chaotic would be an understatement. While the residents needed help immediately, bringing hope to those who were still there was needed right away . . . and help came. The Greater Holy Temple Church of God in Christ, like other ministries, sought the heart of God, and a vision was birthed to serve the residents who found themselves trapped in a crisis spinning out of control. The role of vision was essential if residents would find hope. Bishop Roger Jones and his wife Sandy

---

13 Merrit Kennedy, "Lead-Laced Water in Flint: A Step-by-Step Look at the Makings of a Crisis," *NPR*, 20 Apr. 2016, www.npr.org/sections/thetwo-way/2016/04/20/465545378/lead-laced-water-in-flint-a-step-by-step-look-at-the-makings-of-a-crisis.

14 Kennedy, "Lead-Laced Water . . ."

15 Kennedy, "Lead-Laced Water . . ."

16 Kennedy, "Lead-Laced Water . . ."

responded to the most immediate crisis, providing clean water.[17] Every day, their church was on the frontline of ministry. Thousands of bottles of water were provided.

Bishop Roger and Sandy went as far as they could see at the moment, and that step of faith led to a new vision for expanded ministry. They discovered that not only were they responding to contaminated water, they soon discovered that Flint was a food desert. The quality of food would have a profound impact on residents' ability to maintain good health. This burden birthed a new food ministry. Then, another problem surfaced. The church's food ministry, soon in partnership with other agencies, discovered that many of those they sought to assist had no transportation to pick up the food they so desperately needed. This birthed a partnership with city transportation systems to bring people to the distribution site, and more drivers were hired. This amazing partnership began with the desire to distribute clean water, but other needs prompted a bigger vision for food distribution. That's how visions grow.

The backstory through all of this is that the people of Flint have had to drink bottled water for almost a decade. Their home values have plummeted because no one wants to buy a house where the water isn't safe to drink. And more than that, as many as fourteen thousand children are developmentally delayed because of exposure to high levels of lead in their water.[18] The Flint water disaster unfolded in slow motion: from a seemingly smart decision to save money on the city's water, to ignored complaints, to falsified testing, to government malfeasance, to the nuisance of having to use bottled water, and the result of physical harm to thousands of children in the city. The justice department eventually identified individuals and held them responsible, but for most of that time and while most of the damage was done, faceless bureaucracies failed miserably. The entire system of government was to blame.

THE COURAGE OF A LION

It would be hard to find a better example of someone who doggedly stood against injustice than Dr. Martin Luther King, Jr. His campaign to drag the country out of Jim Crow segregation and into the light of a new world of equality required enormous

17 Stacy Swimp, "Bishop Roger Jones: No One Should Have a Second without Hope," *The HUB Flint*, 13 Jan. 2018, www.thehubflint.com/bishop-roger-jones-no-one-should-have-a-second-without-hope/.

18 "Early Results from 174 Flint Children Exposed to Lead during Water Crisis Shows 80% of Them Will Require Special Education Services," *CBS News*, 15 Mar. 2020, www.cbsnews.com/news/flint-water-crisis-effect-on-children-60-minutes-2020-03-15/.

courage and tenacity. We usually pick up his story during the Montgomery bus boycott that began in 1955. Before Rosa Parks refused to go to the back, fifteen-year-old Claudette Colvin refused to give up her seat for a white man. Both of these cases led to the boycott, which lasted more than a year. Dr. King, not long out of seminary, led the boycott because other ministers declined the role. During the tense and hate-filled year, Dr. King's house was bombed, and he was arrested. The boycott ended only when the United States District Court ruled that racial segregation was prohibited on all Montgomery buses.

Dr. King was active during the next several years in the founding of the Southern Christian Leadership Conference and the Gandhi Society for Human Rights, both advocating nonviolence as the means to enact social change in America. He believed peaceful protests against discriminatory Jim Crow laws would garner media coverage, which would shift the perspective of people throughout the country—even in the South.

The pivotal year for the movement was 1963. The SCLC launched a campaign against segregation and economic inequality in Birmingham, Alabama. Perhaps the most famous images in the entire Civil Rights Movement are of Police Chief Bull Connor unleashing snarling dogs and water canon on the peaceful protesters. Of course, King was arrested, and he wrote his famous and moving "Letter from Birmingham Jail," in which he responded to criticism that agitation was having a detrimental impact on people across the South. He confronted their belief that time would remedy the injustices:

> I must make two honest confessions to you, my Christian and Jewish brothers. First, I must confess that over the past few years I have been gravely disappointed with the white moderate. I have almost reached the regrettable conclusion that the Negro's great stumbling block in his stride toward freedom is not the White Citizen's Counciler or the Ku Klux Klanner, but the white moderate, who is more devoted to "order" than to justice; who prefers a negative peace which is the absence of tension to a positive peace which is the presence of justice; who constantly says: "I agree with you in the goal you seek, but I cannot agree with your methods of direct action"; who paternalistically believes he can set the timetable for another man's freedom; who lives by a mythical concept of time and who constantly advises the

Negro to wait for a "more convenient season." Shallow understanding from people of good will is more frustrating than absolute misunderstanding from people of ill will. Lukewarm acceptance is much more bewildering than outright rejection.[19]

On a hot summer day, Wednesday, August 23, 1968, Rev. Dr. Martin Luther King, Jr. stood on the steps of the Lincoln Memorial to deliver his speech to 250,000 people, and, yes, the world. But he didn't just deliver a speech—he stood as an artist to paint on the canvas of a new tomorrow, a new tomorrow for everyone in America. Stroke by stroke, he painted a picture of life in a just society. Stroke by stroke, he painted clearly, so the audience (including us) can see "little black boys and black girls joining hands with little white boys and white girls as sisters and brothers."[20]

That wouldn't be the only time Dr. King painted on the canvas. On Monday night, April 3, 1968, in Mason Temple, the World Headquarters of the Church of God in Christ, he picked up the brush again. He carefully painted what would be his last picture on the canvas of America's tomorrow: It's all right to talk about "long white robes over yonder," in all of its symbolism. But ultimately people want some suits and dresses and shoes to wear down here. It's all right to talk about "streets flowing with milk and honey," but God has commanded us to be concerned about the slums down here, and his children who can't eat three square meals a day. It's all right to talk about the new Jerusalem, but one day, God's preachers must talk about the New York, the new Atlanta, the new Philadelphia, the new Los Angeles, the new Memphis, Tennessee. This is what we have to do.

Dr. King, finished his artistic painting of tomorrow with a few final strokes that cannot be erased, though some have tried.

Well, I don't know what will happen now. We've got some difficult days ahead. But it doesn't matter with me now. Because I've been to the mountaintop. And I don't mind. Like anybody, I would like to live a long life. Longevity has its place. But I'm not concerned about that now. I just want to do God's will. And He's allowed me to go up to the mountain. And I've looked over. And I've seen the promised land. I may

19 Martin Luther King, Jr., "Letter from the Birmingham Jail," 12 June 1963, https://kinginstitute.stanford.edu/encyclopedia/letter-birmingham-jail.

20 Martin Luther King, Jr., "I Have a Dream," *The Martin Luther King, Jr., Research and Education Institute*, 30 May 2019, kinginstitute.stanford.edu/encyclopedia/i-have-dream.

not get there with you. But I want you to know tonight, that we, as a people, we'll get to the promised land. And I'm happy, tonight. I'm not worried about anything. I'm not fearing any man. "Mine eyes have seen the glory of the coming of the Lord!"[21]

With those words, in our modern vernacular, we would say he "dropped the mic." Or should we say, he "dropped the brush." On the next day, April 4, at the Loraine Hotel in Memphis, Tennessee, he was assassinated. His life came to an end . . . or did it? The artist is gone, but is it possible that his canvas of tomorrow lives on in our country, encouraging some and haunting others? Over the years, I have been privileged to go to Memphis and stand behind the same pulpit where Dr. King stood—but never without thinking of the canvas he left us.

Dr. King was a man of action—peaceful, respectful action, but action designed to remedy the age-old scourge of racism and injustice. In this letter, he explained, "Injustice anywhere is a threat to justice everywhere. We are caught in an inescapable network of mutuality, tied in a single garment of destiny. Whatever affects one directly, affects all indirectly."[22] He stood tall against the powers that had intimidated his people for centuries. It cost him his freedom more than a dozen times when he was arrested, and eventually, it cost him his life when he was assassinated. Through it all, he was resolute in his faith and courage.

CREATIVE SOLUTIONS TO A FLAWED SYSTEM

From the earliest days of Glad Tidings, God gave us a vision to reclaim and restore the community, not just focus on the people who came to church on Sunday mornings. Seeing young men going to jail was never our intent or desire. God had a plan for every person on the street, and my heart's desire has been to help them discover that plan and see themselves in light of God's tomorrow. Today, the prayer ministry for Glad Tidings has been going for more than forty years, Tuesday through Friday, at 9:00 a.m. Not long after the church was launched, we were in our new facility, but we weren't yet in the new sanctuary. We were using the fellowship hall for our prayer gatherings. One morning, as we prayed, I sensed an urging to go out and claim the property that was next door to our new church. The property included four houses

---

21 Dr. Martin Luther King, Jr., "I've Been to the Mountaintop," 3 Apr. 1968, https://www.afscme.org/about/history/mlk/mountaintop.

22 King, "Letter from the Birmingham Jail."

that were in complete disrepair on one large lot. Each of the modest, two-bedroom, one-bath homes was being used for a different drug of choice. It was a dangerous place indeed. No one dared to walk between those buildings, unless he was doing business there. A large tent had been set up on the lawn. Motorcycles were parked nearby, and pit bulls were tied to stakes. It was frightening.

I remember walking by the property with the police chief one day. I said, "Come on, let's go up in here, Chief." He paused and stood at the sidewalk. He wasn't in a hurry to get near that place. I said to him, "Chief, it's okay. I know them." We walked a few more steps, but he wasn't willing to walk any farther. That tells you something about the inherent danger of being on this property! We wanted the land, but we had no idea how to get it.

That morning, I sensed within my spirit that it was time to move forward. I got off my knees and went to look at the property. Standing on the outside, I made phone calls to real estate agents to find someone who represented the owner. Sure enough, we found the agent for the property. I called him and said, "Sir, I'm Reverend Macklin. We've just bought the property next door to the four houses, and we'd like to purchase this property as well."

He said, "Sir, hold on just a minute, please. I'm sure the owners want to sell."

I soon discovered that most of the people who lived on the property were illegal and refused to pay rent. They threatened the property manager if he said anything to the police or Immigration and Customs Enforcement, commonly known as ICE.

The agent made a few phone calls to the owners and asked if they'd agree to sell. Soon, he called back and asked, "Rev. Macklin, when would you like to close on the property?" If my memory serves me well, we only had to take over the existing payments on the loan. Somehow, God blessed us to do the deal, and before long, we owned all four houses.

After the church had acquired the property, we had to figure out how to take possession of it. How do we move people from this property who were undocumented? It was quite a fight. We went door to door to meet them, tell them we were the new owners, and reason with them. We explained, "You're going to have to move. You can't stay here any longer. The church owns this property now." They didn't have leases anyway; it was more of a cash-in-hand arrangement. They were reluctant to leave, and it was very unsettling.

The last property we took possession of was the house on the right—there were three houses on the left and a driveway in between. I knocked on the door, and the young man looked at me and said, "Sir, I'm not going nowhere, and you can't make me!"

I told him plainly, "Young man, you've got to get out of here. The church owns this property now, and you have to move. This property is God's property, and you must move."

I could tell he was high. I looked at him, and he looked at me. He reached over and picked up a can of gasoline, (what he was doing with that gas in the house, I don't know) and poured it on the carpet where I stood. He reached into his pocket and pulled out a match and struck it. He held it up in front of me and snarled, "I'll blow this place up!"

I looked directly into his eyes and said calmly, "I'm ready to go to heaven, sir. What about you?"

Instantly, he blew out the match, fell on my shoulder, and with tears streaming down his face, he cried, "Reverend, all I want to do is get married, get out of here, and get my life together. I don't want to live like this!"

I said, "Son, we're going to help you."

At that point, he told me more of his life's story, and I knew that he was too hot to put on the street. Gangs had a hit out on him, and he wouldn't live another day. I called my dear friend, Pastor Steve Pineda from Victory Outreach, and explained what was going on. I told Steve that I wanted to find a home for a man living in the house we'd bought, but he couldn't stay in the Bay Area because I was sure he wouldn't live to tell about it. Steve responded, "Wait a minute. I'll make a call." Steve called their men's home in Visalia in the Central Valley. Only a few hours later, the young man was on a bus. He stayed there for several months until he got his life together. The Lord touched him. He had a change of heart and change of direction.

When he came back, he looked like a new person. He found me right away and excitedly exclaimed, "Reverend, I'm back!"

I said, "I see you. I'm so happy for you!"

He said, "I want to get married to my girlfriend, but I don't have any money. I don't know what to do."

I asked, "Can you afford a marriage license?" He nodded, so I explained, "Get a marriage license, and come back. I'll give you a wedding right here. I'll have one of our people prepare food. They'll make your wedding cake, and we will do it all here at the church."

We scheduled the wedding for three or four days later. We decorated the old chapel of the church and prepared for the wedding. He came back with a marriage license, his fiancé, his family, and a few friends. I performed the ceremony. He was so happy. At the reception, he looked at me and said, "I can't pay you, but thank you."

I smiled and replied, "You're welcome! It's my pleasure."

After the wedding and the reception, he and his bride left the church, and I've never seen that young man again. I didn't think much of it after he was gone. I was just grateful that we had the four houses and could begin the transition to restore them.

I didn't think of the man and his new wife very often . . . until we worked with the property directly across the street from us, which would later become known as the Cobden Lot. The Cobden property belonged to an elderly gentleman who had been living there since the early twenties. By this time, the property was a disaster area. It had about twenty old cars sitting in the back covered in mud, rusted and inoperable. In addition, there was antiquated equipment in the yard and an old, dilapidated house. The property was in dire need of attention.

The city had sent letters to pressure Mr. Cobden to clean it up, but he was determined to ignore them. Then, we got involved. At a gathering of the men of our church, I explained the situation and the need to clean up our neighbor's lot. I invited the men to join me: "Let's do it!" We hired a tow truck to remove all of the cars, which proved to be an all-day project. We started at 10 a.m. and finished around 10 p.m. After all the cars were towed and the equipment moved across the street, I asked the tow truck driver what we owed him. He responded, "Pastor, you don't owe me anything,"

"Sir, you've been working all day." I replied. "We have to pay you something. Just tell us, and we'll pay you."

He looked at me, and he said, "You don't remember me, but I was in your church a few years ago for a wedding. My son had been strung out on drugs and all messed up, and you helped him. You got him out of that house." He paused for a second and then told me, "You were instrumental in helping him straighten out his life. When he came back, you married him and his girlfriend. Now, they're doing fine. They live in Oregon, and I have a little grandbaby. All of this time, I've been waiting to say thank you, to tell you how much I appreciate what you did for my son. So, Pastor, you don't owe me anything. Thank you."

He got in his truck and drove away. Tears filled my eyes, and even now, I can't talk about it too long without thinking about the healed leper who came back to say, "Thank you" to Jesus.

All leaders, and especially pastors, have to address the unseen, often unidentified, but very real powers of systems and mindsets that keep our people locked into either hopelessness or unrealistic (and ungodly) demands for political power over others. We can throw up our hands and complain that there's nothing we can do about it, or we can do the hard work of identifying the dark powers and taking action to remedy injustice wherever we find it. Sometimes we'll need to go to city hall to protest and ask for changes, and sometimes, our efforts will lead us to someone who has been caught up in those dark powers, so we can share the love of Jesus and see God transform a life.

At the end of Paul's magnificent chapter in the middle of his letter to the Romans, he's realistic about the struggles all of us face in a flawed and fallen world, but it's not hopeless, and we're not helpless. I can almost hear him shout:

> *For I am persuaded that neither death nor life, nor angels nor principalities nor powers, nor things present nor things to come, nor height nor depth, nor any other created thing, shall be able to separate us from the love of God which is in Christ Jesus our Lord.* —*Romans 8:38-39*

Nehemiah waded in to change the broken system and restore hope to the hopeless. It required every ounce of leadership skill he possessed, and God used him to do what no one imagined could happen.

God is looking to you to change unjust systems and the toxic mindsets of the people around you, too. Are you ready?

CONSIDER THIS:

1) What are some injustices that disgust or anger you? (You might think of disproportionate police shootings of Black people, inequality in wealth and education, polarization in politics, leaders who commit sexual offenses, and many others.)

2) How would you define and describe "learned helplessness"? How big of a problem is it in the lives of people you know?

3) Do you agree or disagree with the idea that injustice is such a big problem that there's really nothing you can do about it? Explain your answer.

4) What are some injustices and toxic mindsets you can identify close to home—maybe *in* your home?

5) If you had the resources, how would you address these?

6) Where can you put your hands on those resources?

7) What is God saying to you in this chapter? What actions will you take right away?

WORD ON THE STREET

ERIC SWALWELL

United States Congressman, California's 15th District

When I began my first campaign for Congress in 2011, I wanted to meet leaders in our district. I grew up and lived in the Tri Valley area, "on the other side of the hill" from Hayward. I asked a number of people in Hayward who I should meet to talk about my candidacy, and Bishop Macklin's name came up again and again. It wasn't easy to meet him because he was so busy, but I met his son, and he took me to a festival at Glad Tidings. There, he introduced me to his father. By that time, I'd heard so much about the Bishop that I expected him to be ten feet tall! I was a little nervous because his support carried so much weight in the area around his church, and in fact, throughout the city. He was very gracious to listen to me make my case, and he wanted to be sure I understood what the community needed from government. Telling me wasn't enough; he took me on a guided tour of the neighborhood. He explained how resources had been invested and made a difference, but he also told me how much more needed to be done. I was learning from the expert.

During my first year in Washington, I invited Bishop Macklin to open a daily session in prayer. He stood at the same lectern where the President speaks when he gives the State of the Union Address. I'm sure he felt it was an honor to pray for the country and our work that day, and it was an honor for me to have him there.

Our friendship has grown over the years, and it has been a privilege to be his co-conspirator in many important projects. I could list dozens, but let me highlight two: When Obamacare passed and became available, I asked Bishop Macklin to host an event to sign up people in the community, and to have resource people available to speak in many languages, so we could serve everybody. He brought in a number of service organizations, so they could participate in signing people up for the Affordable Care Act. It was a very successful event.

More recently, as the vaccine became available to fight Covid, a local FEMA administrator asked me to help him find a location where he could create a mobile vaccination site. He hoped the site could serve at least five hundred people. I called Bishop Macklin, and he was happy to open the doors of the Glad Tidings campus on a Saturday and Sunday. They vaccinated over one thousand people. This was even more significant because the African American community is understandably hesitant due to the horrific medical abuse in Tuskegee for decades in the last century. The Bishop's leadership calmed nerves and gave assurance that the vaccine is safe and effective.

Bishop Macklin is known as the consummate activist—he gets things done. Whenever I ask him for help, he dives in and makes it happen, but he isn't grim about his calling. He has a wonderful, deep laugh, and he has been known to cut a rug during church services. I appreciate how he honors his wife Vanessa, and he dearly loves his children. He has imparted his compassion and values to them, so they can follow in his footsteps. He's a remarkable visionary, a gifted leader, a valued partner, and a dear friend. I love being around him.

CHAPTER 9

GOOD TROUBLE AHEAD

Nehemiah Endured When Others Would Have Given Up

G od's people, by the thousands, had become comfortable living among the ruins. Demoralized, they had lost hope for something better. And now an aide to the king had waltzed in with the grand plan to rebuild the walls? Who had he said he was? And who did he think he was? Nehemiah hadn't come to Jerusalem with a business card and a business plan; he'd come with a colorful, vibrant, breathtaking picture painted on a canvas marked tomorrow. He was a visionary, a leader, and a representative of God.

We've already seen that Nehemiah faced fierce opposition from the beginning of and throughout the building process. When his workers were physically threatened by Ammonite and Ashdodite forces, he didn't panic, but he didn't ignore the threat. He had half of the workers stand as armed guards while the others worked, and even those who kept working had a sword in one hand and a tool in the other. (Ambidextrous, don't you think?)

Nehemiah expands on this scene:

> *Speaking to the nobles, the rulers, and the rest of the people, "The work is great and extensive, and we are separated far from one another on the wall. Wherever*

you hear the sound of the trumpet, rally to us there. Our God will fight for us." So we labored in the work, and half of the men held the spears from daybreak until the stars appeared. At the same time I also said to the people, "Let each man and his servant stay at night in Jerusalem, that they may be our guard by night and a working party by day." —Nehemiah 4:19-23

Was the work hard? Yes.

Were the threats real? Certainly.

Did people complain? Undoubtedly.

Did Nehemiah waver? Never.

His endurance was a product of several essential factors: He was emotionally invested with compassion for the people of Jerusalem, God had given him a vision to restore the walls to protect the people and restore their sense of security and dignity, God had a track record of faithfulness in supplying the resources for the task at hand. Nehemiah's detailed plan involved putting people to work where their homes would be protected, and he responded to each difficulty with that kind of wisdom.

Chapter 3 in Nehemiah's account is a study in organizational excellence. Families were assigned to particular sections of the wall and specific gates, and all the timber and stones were secured, so there would be no delays in construction. Titles and previous job descriptions didn't mean much. The success of the project required the people to follow Nehemiah's instructions to the tee. In a fascinating sentence, Nehemiah wrote, "Next to him Uzziel the son of Harhaiah, one of the goldsmiths, made repairs. Also next to him Hananiah, one of the perfumers, made repairs; and they fortified Jerusalem as far as the Broad Wall" (Nehemiah 3:8). The goldsmith didn't say, "I'm not getting my hands dirty and calloused by handling those big, rough stones!" The perfumer didn't protest, "This work just doesn't fit my career profile. Besides, the people I'd have to work with smell bad!" No, they rolled up their sleeves and went to work wherever Nehemiah assigned them.

Nehemiah wasn't a quitter. He didn't ignore Hanani when he heard the report about Jerusalem, and he didn't hesitate to ask the king for permission and resources. When he arrived in Jerusalem, he didn't quit when he saw the enormity of the task before him, and he didn't cower when he faced opposition. After the threats from outsiders, Nehemiah and his workers were threatened by insiders—which is usually much more devastating. As the wall was being constructed, Jewish elites insisted on receiving food even though they refused to work—and they demanded payment from the workers for the food they'd purchased from the elites. You can imagine the outrage among the laborers! Nehemiah would have nothing of it:

> *And I became very angry when I heard their outcry and these words. After serious thought, I rebuked the nobles and rulers, and said to them, "Each of you is exacting usury from his brother." So I called a great assembly against them. And I said to them, "According to our ability we have redeemed our Jewish brethren who were sold to the nations. Now indeed, will you even sell your brethren? Or should they be sold to us?" Then they were silenced and found nothing to say.*

But Nehemiah wasn't finished. He gave them an ultimatum:

> *Then I said, "What you are doing is not good. Should you not walk in the fear of our God because of the reproach of the nations, our enemies? I also, with my brethren and my servants, am lending them money and grain. Please, let us stop this usury! Restore now to them, even this day, their lands, their vineyards, their olive groves, and their houses, also a hundredth of the money and the grain, the new wine and the oil, that you have charged them."*
>
> *So they said, "We will restore it, and will require nothing from them; we will do as you say."*
>
> *Then I called the priests, and required an oath from them that they would do according to this promise. Then I shook out the fold of my garment and said, "So may God shake out each man from his house, and from his property, who does not perform this promise. Even thus may he be shaken out and emptied."*
>
> *And all the assembly said, "Amen!" and praised the LORD. Then the people did according to this promise. —Nehemiah 5:6-13*

In the end, Nehemiah's endurance—along with God's provision and the work of His people—accomplished something truly extraordinary. They completed the wall in only fifty-two days! Now the tables were turned: God's people felt encouraged and vindicated, and His enemies "were very disheartened in their own eyes, for they perceived that this work was done by our God" (Nehemiah 6:16).

Organization had been key to Nehemiah's success. We get a similar glimpse of the value of organization when Jesus saw that people who had been listening to Him preach were hungry and far from the nearest food truck. We're familiar with the story told in Matthew 14:13-21, but it helps to take a look at it from a slightly different point of view, an organizational perspective:

» Jesus recognized a need—He was "moved with compassion" because the people were hungry.

» He realized the predicament—The disciples' plan to send the people to nearby villages for food wasn't a workable option, so He directed them differently.

» He identified the available resources—The disciples found a boy whose sack lunch had five little fish and two small loaves.

» He took possession of the resources—He told them, "Bring them here to Me."

» He gave instructions for people to sit in manageable groups—They could be fed more readily this way.

» He asked the Father to bless the meal—Jesus knew that the Father wasn't limited by what looked to be an inadequate supply of resources.

» He delegated responsibility to the disciples—They became the wait-staff at the feast.

» He passed out food until everyone had eaten their fill—No stomachs growled.

» He oversaw the cleanup and the reallocation of leftover resources—Twelve basketsful remained.

Those who benefitted from the meal were five thousand men plus women and children, probably about twenty thousand altogether. It was one of the most memorable miracles in the Gospels, and it happened because two things came together at the same time: the power of God and effective organization.

HOLY WEEK: MARCH ON!

Like most churches, Holy Week at Glad Tidings is revival time. We wanted to provide a powerful, life-changing experience through reflective thought, fasting, and spiritual renewal. Although we were giving God praise for our newly erected sanctuary, we were aware that, while improving, the neighborhood was still plagued with tension, violence, and drugs. We weren't finished, and in fact, we'd only begun to impact the negative culture of South Hayward. In preparation for our Holy Week observance, the Lord directed me to a passage of scripture that I'd been taught and read hundreds of times from my youth. I could still recall what our Sunday school teacher taught us in our card class: Joshua fought the battle of Jericho. Once again, I opened the Bible to read it, only this time, as so often is the case, I saw Glad Tidings in the text.

> *And the Lord said to Joshua: "See! I have given Jericho into your hand, its king, and the mighty men of valor. You shall march around the city, all you men of war; you shall go all around the city once. This you shall do six days. And seven priests shall bear seven trumpets of rams' horns before the ark. But the seventh day you shall march around the city seven times, and the priests shall blow the trumpets. It shall come to pass, when they make a long blast with the ram's horn, and when you hear the sound of the trumpet, that all the people shall shout with a great shout; then the wall of the city will fall down flat. And the people shall go up every man straight before him." —Joshua 6:2-5*

In previous readings of this passage, I'd seen Israel walking, but now I could see Glad Tidings walking. Like God's people generations earlier, we had come out of Egypt and crossed the Red Sea into a new place, but the battle was far from over. Jericho stood in our way. I announced to the church two weeks before Holy Week, "This year, I want you to join me as we march around this neighborhood. Starting Monday night of Holy Week, we'll march around this one square block one time every evening this week. And on Friday night, we'll march around this block seven times. After the seventh time, we'll shout, and God will bring the walls down!" I was sure they understood I was speaking metaphorically.

Like Nehemiah, the instructions were specific, to be followed to the letter. We would march two by two in total silence. We were to speak to no one—not reporters, police, or neighbors. No one. The sound of silence would fill the streets for all to hear.

Every evening that week, men, women, and youth gathered by the hundreds at the front doors of the church on the corner of Tyrrell Avenue and began our loud silent march. Although I was at the front of the march, I wasn't leading the procession. We followed a fiery torch on a pole. With the torch brightly lit and held high, we walked in absolute silence.

Months earlier, a move of God was taking place in an unusual setting: the Oakland Raiders football team. In a Bible study with the wives of NFL players, God was changing lives. Chester McGlockton, an Oakland Raiders superstar, had married a young lady from our church. Another player had given his life to Christ, and his life was turned in a new direction. Tim Brown and his family were already committed believers, and he was a big encouragement to them both, showing up faithfully to Glad Tidings with tambourine in hand to give God praise.

On the first night of our march, dressed in his athletic attire, Terry stepped forward and asked, "Pastor, can I lead the march and carry the torch?" Looking at the big, strong NFL player and then myself, the answer wasn't difficult: "Yes, we'll follow you!"

The march was on, and our orders were clear. Every evening, with our marching shoes on, we began with prayer, and then we started walking two by two in silence. Neighbors looked on, children rode bicycles in the streets, and voices shouted, "What y'all doing?" "Where y'all going?" "What's happening?" "What's up?" Our response was the same for every question: total silence. Not a word—only the sound of shoes hitting the pavement. At other times in the history of our church, we've preached on the street with megaphones and PA systems, but our voices had never been louder and more piercing than when we preached without uttering a word. The deafening silence could be heard for blocks, and it was incredible.

By the second night, police cars were circling the block. The officers weren't sure of our intentions. They witnessed hundreds of African Americans and other people of color marching in lockstep, like a well-disciplined regiment. We broke no laws. We walked only on the sidewalk. The torch and our presence communicated loudly and clearly, "Jesus Christ is Lord in the house and on the street!"

By the third night, the number of marching saints grew even larger. As we turned the corner toward the church, an older African American mother watched the torch come her way. She stood on her balcony watching us march two by two, in silence behind the torch. Suddenly, she shouted loudly, to who knows whom, "The Reverend told y'all to stop selling them drugs! Now he's going to burn this whole town down!"

Not a word had been spoken from Sunday to Thursday. By the end of each evening's march of silence, men and women entered the sanctuary and prayed to God, who was giving us strength. Only God could lead us to joyfully and expectantly walk on the streets that had been filled with violence, death, and destruction. People in our neighborhood cowered in fear as gangs controlled every movement. No human being or governmental agency could change the status quo. The neighborhood could only be challenged and changed through the power of the Holy Spirit.

It was clear by now that no one knew our intentions. When Friday came, like Joshua and his army, we marched in silence once again. It was an unbelievable sight.

The saints of God were determined to complete the assignment. We were on the wall, and we weren't coming down. Once around, then twice, a third time, a fourth, fifth, and sixth. Each time, the saints had renewed strength and resolve. Then, as we began our seventh circuit, we could tell something was about to happen. It was as if the street were shaking beneath our feet. As the torch began the final round, the voices of the saints would finally be heard, and heard they were! As we approach the church, completing our seventh time around that night, a shout went up as one voice, "Hallelujah! Hallelujah! Hallelujah!" It was overwhelming. The sound seemed to last forever. We were experiencing the joy of a Psalm 47 moment:

> *Oh, clap your hands, all you peoples! Shout to God with the voice of triumph!* —*Psalm 47:1-2*

There was dancing, crying, and hugging in the street. We were sure our neighborhood would never be the same. Within moments, we saw doors to apartments swing open, and people ran out with hands raised, some asking for prayer and others asking God to save them. It was a God Moment like I'd never seen before.

We weren't with Joshua when the walls of Jericho came down, but this night we felt a connection, a spiritual breakthrough on the street. Yes, our God reigns! Believers and non-believers alike knew, without a doubt, that God was on His throne. Glad Tidings understood that the square footage of your building, the length of your aisles, or the width of your pews does not determine the size of your church. The size of your church is measured by the size of your vision.

EARNING THE RIGHT TO BE HEARD

Being heard doesn't come from titles, positions, loudspeakers, or flyers on doors. To be heard "for real," you must earn that right.

Here are the questions people inherently (if silently) ask about us:

- » "Who are you?"
- » "Where did you come from?"
- » "How long have you been here? You think I care what you think?"
- » "Are you planning to leave after you make your noise?"
- » "Are you for us or against us?"
- » "I know you see us now, but how do you see us in the future?"
- » "Is this only a photo op or a publicity stunt for you? If it is, we've seen it all before, and we're not interested."

One block north of our front doors, there was a notorious cul-de-sac known as Harris Court. People didn't live there out of desire but desperation. It was their last choice. It was a place of extreme poverty, and violence was a daily occurrence. If you wanted to go to heaven, show up on any given Saturday night, and you could get a one-way ticket. One particular weekend was extremely bad: gun shots rang out, bodies were left lying in the street, and the residents were scared, with many shut up in their apartments looking out between the blinds. When I went there to see how I could help, the Lord spoke to my heart—I heard Him so clearly, *You must earn the right to be heard.*

I didn't need to call a three-day fast, a committee meeting, the church council, city officials, or the police department. Within hours, I sounded the trumpet to a church that remained at the ready. This wasn't a time for investigative reporting, but rather, a time to roll up our sleeves and go to work: we got our pickup trucks, rakes, shovels, brooms, water hoses, and large trash bags. We knew what had to be done. The circle where people lived was covered in trash, overgrown weeds, garbage, and all matter of debris. Without asking for permission, Team GT was on the case, and we went to work. With 40 to 50 volunteers working together with joy and love, something magnificent happened! Some worked while others prayed. (Thanks for the leadership tip, Nehemiah!) The driveways and fronts of homes were clean for the first time in . . . well, a long time. People peered out of their windows not sure what was happening.

With the street cleaned, I jumped on the back of a flatbed, and with a megaphone in hand, shouted for all to hear, "I'm Pastor Jerry Macklin, and we're your neighbors from Glad Tidings Church. We've just cleaned up this entire area, and we've earned the right to be heard!" I went on to say, "Open your windows and your doors, and walk out onto your porches. I want to speak to you for a few minutes. You deserve better, and God has better for you." I took time to describe God's tomorrow canvas. "You're important to God, and you're important to us. We can do better! We will do better!"

I preached for a few minutes more, and then I invited anyone who wanted us to pray for them to walk out to the sidewalk where people were waiting to pray for them and their families. From that day forward, there was a change in Harris Court. No, all of the problems weren't solved. Poverty wasn't eliminated, and there would still be violent acts on occasion, but it was never again as bad as it had been. Hope had been ignited, and the glorious gospel of Christ had been seen and felt. Yes, we had earned the right to be heard! The Harris Court cul-de-sac has since undergone a transformative makeover with new and remodeled apartments. Those who live there now have little knowledge of the night we came.

Transforming a community requires a longtime commitment. You don't do the work just to be seen, but by all means, you should be seen doing the work. Day by day, week by week, year by year, it's important to do the hard work. Quite often, people thank us for caring and helping, but sometimes, we get angry stares and unkind words. Although we've been honored by city and county governments, the US Senate and Congress, and even the White House, we are not motivated for ministry for personal recognition. We're just following Jesus to care for those who are less fortunate, to provide tangible, physical resources, and represent Him in the best way we can. We have come to understand that there are many who are not broke, but they are broken. Jesus has come for the down-and-out, and Jesus has come for the up-and-out. Zacchaeus, come down. Jesus wants to go home with you today. After all, it makes no difference who gets the credit as long as God gets the glory.

CONSIDER THIS:

1) How would you describe the connection between endurance and organization? How does one affect the other?

2) If you'd been one of Nehemiah's workers, how would you have felt when he told you to keep working but keep a sword in your hand?

3) And how would you have felt when the wall was completed? How would you feel about those who worked beside you?

   . . . the Jewish nobles who refused to work?

   . . . Sanballat and Tobiah?

   . . . and Nehemiah?

4) Can you imagine participating in a weeklong march in silence around your community?

5) What impact might it have on you, your family, and your church? What impact might it have on your neighbors who observe it all?

6) What are other creative ways your church can move into the community to make a difference?

7) What activities can you initiate?

8) What are some organizations you can partner with to make an impact?

9) What are five specific ways you can earn the right to be heard?

10) Which of them are you already doing? Which ones need some energy and creativity to make them happen?

11) What is God saying to you in this chapter? What are the struggles in which you need to endure?

WORD ON THE STREET

FREDDYE DAVIS

*Former President and Chief Spokesperson for the
Hayward and Alameda County NAACP*

I met Bishop Macklin about forty years ago when he arrived in Hayward. He put a sign in front of the church announcing its opening, and many of us went to the church to welcome him to the community. I could tell he was a true man of God. From the beginning, he told us that he loved God and he loved the community, and he would do everything possible to help people. Needless to say, he has been true to his word.

When he arrived, the area around the church was infested with drugs. I watched Bishop Macklin engage with the drug dealers, telling them that God loved them and explaining that God had a better life and future for them. He earned the respect of most of them, but at least on one occasion (that I know about), his life was threatened. His love changed attitudes and hearts, and his civic engagement made the neighborhood a desirable place to live.

He was a vital part of everything the NAACP tried to do in the community, always ready to lend a hand, take leadership, and provide resources to care for people. He has done so much to promote racial equality and fair treatment of people of color. I remember a Black man who had been surrounded by police officers. The confrontation was tense and about to escalate further when Bishop Macklin happened to come by. He stepped in to lower the level of suspicion and animosity, and the confrontation ended in a peaceful outcome.

In his community revitalization, he made sure to care for the homeless population. He worked hard to help them find clean, low-cost housing as they learned a trade and found jobs. For many people, the direction of their lives changed, and for the first time, they had a sense of hope for the future. For those who didn't have enough to eat, Glad Tidings opened their kitchen several days a week to feed them.

On Thanksgivings, he opened the church to those who had no family nearby, so they could enjoy a good meal with others in the neighborhood. The staff of the church served and treated people like royalty. The tables were set with fine china, silverware, and crystal, with flowers as centerpieces. This wasn't just a way to get food to people in need. It was that, but so much more. People felt loved and valued, maybe for the first time in a long time.

At Christmas, the people of Glad Tidings bought toys for children who wouldn't have gotten anything. After dinner and a program, smartly dressed Santa Claus and Mrs. Claus gave presents to the children. They were delighted, and their parents were very grateful.

The Bishop has always been available to jump in to meet any need, and the community has had plenty of needs. He has been a wonderful partner to the NAACP and a hero in the neighborhood. For his love and hard work to transform the community, the City of Hayward honored him with the Humanitarian and Lifetime Achievement Award. He certainly deserved it. I'm glad to be counted among his friends.

CHAPTER 10

THE STONE THE BUILDERS REJECTED

Nehemiah Declared What Others Had Forgotten

N ehemiah may have lived a comfortable life as the cupbearer in King Artaxerxes's court, but he was a phenomenal leader when God called him to rebuild the walls of Jerusalem. He had a big vision, he had a clear organization, and he spoke powerfully to every segment of the community, friend and foe alike. We've seen how he inspired the workmen, how he confronted their two biggest opponents, and how he rebuked the Jewish elite who tried to take advantage of the situation, so they could profit from it.

When the wall was completed, Nehemiah didn't go on television to brag about his accomplishments, and he didn't post pictures of himself on social media. He didn't try to dominate every news outlet the way many leaders do today. Instead, he pointed the people to the true source of their strength and gave glory to God. Imagine being one of the people in this scene. God had worked wonders among you. You'd been on the wall for more than seven weeks, working hard and carrying a sword. Many times you wondered if the job could possibly be completed, and Nehemiah had assured you that God was in it. Now, weeks after the last stone was put in place, he called everyone to gather together for a special service:

> *Now all the people gathered together as one man in the open square that was in front of the Water Gate; and they told Ezra the scribe to bring the Book of the Law of Moses, which the L*ORD *had commanded Israel. So Ezra the priest brought the Law before the assembly of men and women and all who could hear with under-standing on the first day of the seventh month. Then he read from it in the open square that was in front of the Water Gate from morning until midday, before the men and women and those who could understand; and the ears of all the people were attentive to the Book of the Law....And Ezra opened the book in the sight of all the people, for he was standing above all the people; and when he opened it, all the people stood up. And Ezra blessed the L*ORD*, the great God.*
>
> *Then all the people answered, "Amen, Amen!" while lifting up their hands. And they bowed their heads and worshiped the L*ORD *with their faces to the ground.*
> —*Nehemiah 8:1-3, 5-6*

Those who read the Scriptures "read distinctly from the book, in the Law of God; and they gave the sense, and helped them to understand the reading" (v. 8). In other words, they preached the Word and applied it to their lives! The preaching must have been Spirit-anointed because people were deeply moved. Nehemiah needed to step up and tell the people, "This day is holy to the LORD your God; do not mourn nor weep." For all the people wept, when they heard the words of the Law. Then he said to them, "Go your way, eat the fat, drink the sweet, and send portions to those for whom nothing is prepared; for this day is holy to our Lord. Do not sorrow, for the joy of the LORD is your strength" (vv. 9-10).

Notice that Nehemiah didn't issue a proclamation on his first day in Jerusalem. He didn't have someone read the Scriptures, and no one preached. His first actions were a careful inspection of the broken walls and burned gates, and then he called people to pick up their trowels, shovels, and hammers and join him in the work. In those fifty-two days, Nehemiah earned their respect, earned their trust, and earned the right to be heard. Working side by side with the people of the city and getting his hands as dirty as theirs spoke more loudly than words.

THE JERUSALEM WALL

Like Jerusalem during the exile, our campus needed a wall to ensure our neighbors could live in safety and members could worship in peace. For Nehemiah and his workers, the wall represented the identity, dignity, and strength of the city. Walls in the Bible were structures that protect, gave security and shelter, and provided a sense of belonging. Without walls, cities were open, vulnerable, and quickly approached by enemies who sought to overrun them. On the other hand, the absence of a deterrent sent a loud message to fringe elements and criminal enterprises that products and people were available there.

The back fence that lined many of our recently purchased properties was approximately one thousand linear feet. At the time, most of the fenced areas were in disrepair. Drug dealers and those seeking to escape the law ran over the dilapidated barriers and into people's homes with ease. The openness of our campus was like a neon sign that flashed, "Come on in, and take what you want!" And they did. Drugs were sold on our neighborhood property, and vandalism was a common occurrence. When we asked a city official about building new fences, we received information that they couldn't exceed six feet. We were quick to respond that people looking for shortcuts hurdled six-foot obstacles with ease.

The church launched a project to erect a continuous cement panel wall along the border of all the church-owned adjacent properties. It was a massive endeavor. Neighbors weren't given a bill or asked to contribute to the cost, so we encountered very little resistance from them. Today, the wall stands tall and continues for more than a thousand feet throughout our neighborhood. The new construction earned cheers as the project brought calm and a welcome peace. The wall was appropriately named the "Jerusalem Wall, *Shalom*—Peace."

In our church's history, very few projects have produced such profound results as quickly as this wall—and it has been crucial in our rebranding efforts. This project changed not only our environment but also the expectation of residents. They concluded, "Finally, someone cares about us!"

While the Jerusalem Wall was being built, another wall was also erected—one that needed no permission from the city, no building permits, no city council approval, and no property owner's authorization. This wall had no cost for construction and required no materials. It's invisible to natural eyes, but it was recognized clearly by the Lord Jesus Christ. It's the Wall of Prayer.

Let me make this recommendation to you and your church. Earlier I suggested you use a green pen to mark the neighborhood you want to impact. You might start with one block or one street and begin to walk that street . . . often . . . regularly . . . with your eyes wide open. Yes, walk and pray. You'll be witnessing God at work. Walk and watch the calm that will come. Before long, your neighbors and people on the street will ask you to pray for them.

Just walk and pray. Walk once, twice, or three times a week. Don't stop walking, and don't stop praying. You'll see old walls of suspicion come down and a new wall of love erected. It'll bring joy to your neighbors to know that their families and community are covered in prayer. It will take time, but it's an investment in the identity, dignity, and strength of your community. Our goal was not to see people go to jail or to be imprisoned. Our heart mission is to see people come to know the Lord Jesus and see clearly His plan for their lives. God has a canvas with their name on it.

TURNING ENEMIES INTO FRIENDS

When good and godly actions are coupled with good and godly preaching of God's Word, a culture can be transformed. However, it takes both. Since the days of slavery and Jim Crow, Black people have been suspicious of government authorities—for good reasons! But this lack of trust creates a division that often yields negative results, and it can only be remedied by actions that begin to rebuild trust.

In 1986 a new concept was headed our way, at least, it was new to our city and community: community policing. Would it work here? I wasn't sure, but I knew something needed to change. The crime rate in the city was at its highest, violence was an everyday occurrence, gangs seemed to have free rein, and the streets were an open market for drugs. However, I was convinced that driving through the community with sirens blaring and guns drawn every night wouldn't produce positive results.

Without a doubt, our South Hayward neighborhood was ablaze with hatred, drugs, and guns. There had to be a better way. After many conversations, confrontations, face-to-face dialogues, and on-the-street crisis management, the police chief and I came to an understanding: change was needed and needed now.

The chief of police and I had vastly different concepts of a mobile unit designed to keep peace in the city. Rather than riding through the neighborhood looking like a military platoon at war, I wanted the police to try a different approach: walk, ride bikes, and have meaningful discourse with community residents, giving them the respect they desire and deserve. Instead of sitting in squad cars behind darkened glass, the officers could get out and engage the people in the community. At the police station, the chief could demonstrate consistency by leaving the same teams of officers in place instead of rotating them, so we could get to know them and build trust. If they would sit down with us and listen to us, we could share a desired outcome of peace and safety. I told the chief, "Let's work together. It's no secret that there are plenty of people who don't want peace and safety. They thrive on chaos and hate. These people don't want to see our neighborhood whole." I'd heard more than once, "Pastor, why don't you and Jesus just leave us alone!" (Mark 5:17)

We had to assess the seriousness of the situation: Who has a vested interest in the status quo? Who benefits if things don't change? The winners in the current system were the merchants in the underground economy, unscrupulous property owners, food vendors for prisons, garment vendors, locksmiths, security companies, and of course, pushers, and the suppliers who import products to our community for our young people to sell. How strange that young dealers on the street receive long prison terms and suppliers are seldom convicted or imprisoned.[23]

---

23 "Average Jail Time for Drug Crimes in California," Randy Collins, defense attorney, https://www.drugcrime-law.com/blog/2014/may/average-jail-time-for-drug-crimes-in-california/.

When the city is forced to spend exorbitant amounts of money on patrolling the streets, they have less to spend for positive endeavors. Community policing is asking, "What do we know about our community, schools, rental turnover, homeownership, credit scores, health disparities, high school completion rates, college enrollment and completion, foster care, and welfare? What's working, and what needs to be fixed?"

Do you remember the story I told about a young minister who was also an artist? As he walked in the slums of the city, he saw the man lying in the gutter. The first step of effective community policing, then, was for the officers on patrol to see the needs of the people—instead of seeing them as "the other"—and establish a positive presence in the community. I understood the city budget wouldn't accommodate a formal community policing office, so Glad Tidings would take another approach. We had a small 8 x 10 trailer at the church on Tennyson that was used as a welcome center. We reassigned it to be used as our first neighborhood Community Policing Office. We moved the trailer across the street to our Glad Tidings Park. Police officers working in our neighborhood now had a place to stop, get something to drink, talk with our neighbors, and be refreshed. The CPO provided shade on hot days, and a refrigerator was full of refreshments. The tables and chairs also gave officers a secure and comfortable place to write reports. Most importantly, it was a place where officers could remain visible and available to the youth and adults in the community. We knew it was only a small start, but it was a successful start. Neighborhood tensions were visibly lowered, and lines of communication began to open. From this new launch, the hard work of community-building was off to a great start. Now, officers walked the streets and interacted with people. Together, we were working on the crisis.

We weren't aware that President Bill Clinton's agenda had embraced community policing as a building block for his new administration. The White House had begun a search for a National Community Policing czar. They looked for an inspiring and experienced leader with a track record of success to launch community policing in cities throughout the nation. Little did we know that this search would lead the White House to Hayward, California. Chief Joe Brann, formally of Santa Ana, was a finalist for the position, and Glad Tidings was critical to the search.

I was contacted by a White House representative assigned to the background check of Chief Brann. There were multiple questions and on-site visits. A short time later, we received the news that Chief Brann was on his way to Washington, DC. A few months later, an invitation came from Police Chief Craig Calhoun, who succeeded Chief Joe Brann following his White House promotion. I was being invited as a key presenter for a National Community Policing Conference in the nation's capital. I was honored to attend and present the South Hayward, Glad Tidings Story. Over the years, our Community Policing Office has moved to new and more spacious offices and continues to be successful. When officers and residents get to know each other, sharing joys and concerns, trust is built, tensions subside, and accountability is not avoided—but welcomed. The church must forever be clear; we have been called "to seek the peace of the city" (Jeremiah 29:7).

DECLARING HOPE

Nehemiah declared hope from the moment he took a few men with him on the nightly reconnaissance around the broken walls. He declared hope when he boldly stood up against the threats of Sanballat and Tobiah, and he declared hope when he addressed the nobles' selfishness and injustice in how they treated the workers. He then declared hope by having the Scriptures read and giving glory to God. There are, then, many ways parents, community leaders, and pastors can declare hope. At Glad Tidings, we point people to the goodness and greatness of God every time we get together, in every printed handout, and in every other communication. And we go far beyond what happens on Sunday morning.

In case you haven't gathered by now, South Hayward isn't going to be confused with the Hamptons, Palm Springs, or Nob Hill. It's a disadvantaged community, but it doesn't have to stay that way. To raise the level of possibilities, we invited Silicon Valley to South Hayward.

Empowerment Week

On a weekend, we set up booths, rooms, tents, and any space we could find for representatives of Google, Facebook, Adobe, and the other big tech companies to explain who they are, what they do, and what it takes to find a job there. It was one of the most powerful, positive, successful events we've ever had.

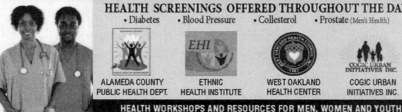

Entrepreneurship Conference

At another time, we planned to host a local conference to encourage entrepreneurs of small businesses. When the idea was still in wet cement, I was at the White House, and I asked President Obama if he could help us with this effort. He replied, "We'll do whatever we can, Bishop!" He pointed to one of his assistants and told him, "Take care of the Bishop." A few months later, we held the event at the church, and hundreds of small business owners came, along with those who were considering starting a business. Sure enough, the President's aide gave us some valuable resources to spur

creativity and enthusiasm among those who attended. People came from all over the area to hear experts explain how to start, grow, and manage a business.

These two events are among many we've held on our campus. We want to minister to the whole person, not just get them a ticket to heaven when they die. Jesus is King

Gerard C. Flavin
Gerard C. Flavin is the assistant administrator at SBA's Center for Faith-Based and Neighborhood Partnerships. This Center works to build strong relationships with both secular and faith-based nonprofit organizations to encourage entrepreneurship, support economic growth and promote prosperity for all Americans.

Valerie Daniels-Carter
Valerie Daniels-Carter, based in Milwaukee, Wisconsin is founder and CEO of V & J Holding Company, Inc., and owner of 137 restaurants with a total $70 billion in sales. She is President and CEO of the country's largest African-American-owned restaurant franchise, and part owner of the NFL Greenbay Packers.

Cedric Grant
Mr. Grant is the Director of the Office of Faith-Based and Neighborhood Partnerships at the Department of Commerce where he forges and enhances partnerships with community and faith-based organizations on policy areas such as community economic development.

What will you learn?
- How to access funds for growing your business
- How to run and grow your business
- New business resources
- CA State University Business Opportunity Program
- Employment Law basics
- Network with other business owners

Employment Workshops
- Learn how to create a winning resume
- Learn how to dress with success
- Learn how to interview successfully
- Learn the importance of the follow up
- And much, much, more

REGISTER ONLINE AT: WWW.GTWORLDIMPACT.COM • CONTINENTAL BREAKFAST, AND LUNCH PROVIDED
Businesses Can Submit 500 Brochures Or Flyers, To Be Distributed To Conference Delegates.
Please Submit All Literature To Glad Tidings Church By April 18, 2012

Host: Elder Lonzo Caves, Director World Impact Ministries
Bishop J.W. Macklin & First Lady Vanessa Macklin

GLAD TIDINGS CHURCH OF GOD IN CHRIST
27689 Tyrrell Avenue, Hayward, CA 94544
510.783.9377 • www.gladtidingscogic.org
Email: worldimpact@gladtidingscogic.org

in their homes, in their wallets, at work, in their hobbies and leisure, and in every other aspect of every single day. And God delights in blessing those who call Him Father and Lord.

SURPRISE

For several years, I made it a priority to read a Stephen Covey leadership book every year. I always found insight and encouragement. In the fall of 2014, I received an invitation to the launch of his book, *The 8th Habit*. After the impact of *7 Habits of*

Highly Effective People, I was sure that his latest release would take it to the next level.
I had never participated in one of his events, but I
decided to go. A few weeks later, I arrived at Sky
Lodge in the mountains of Utah. The four hundred
participants included CEOs, college presidents,
leaders of nonprofits, and corporate administrators.
For the first session, I found a seat on the front row.

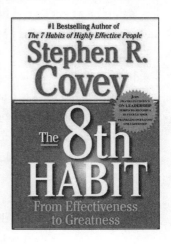

After the first two hours, I knew the conference
would not disappoint. I was writing in our conference workbook when Mr. Covey was preparing to
take a 15-minute break. As he prepared to close the
session, he said, "When we come back, I want to talk
to you about the impact of moral leadership. I'll share a story of a minister who went
to a neighborhood that was overrun with crime and drugs. It was a neighborhood
the police said was the most challenging and dangerous in the city. This minister and
his church moved into the community and, step by step, began community transformation. Week by week and month by month, his church worked in harmony with
community partners, and they saw a dramatic change. What he faced and how he
rose to meet every challenge was amazing. I'll tell you more about this unique story
when we come back." He walked off the stage, and our break began.

I walked over and introduced myself to this leadership legend. "Mr. Covey," I said,
"were you describing a minister in a community in Northern California?"

He responded, "Yes, that's right. Do you know him?"

"Sir, I'm that minister. I'm Bishop Jerry Macklin from Hayward, California."

Mr. Covey just froze, and then we chatted for a few more minutes. Without saying
much more, I returned to my seat, eager for the next session to begin. Mr. Covey
opened this final session before lunch with startling words: "Before the break, I spoke
to you about a minister who went to a city overrun with crime and drugs. Through
his leadership and the work of his church, the community has seen an unbelievable
turnaround. Ladies and gentlemen, that pastor is here with us today. Bishop Macklin, I

want us to exchange places for a short time. Please come and speak to us about moral leadership." As I got up and began walking to the stage, he introduced me, "Ladies and gentlemen, Bishop Jerry Macklin of Hayward, California."

Stephen Covey sat in the front row. For the next thirty minutes, I shared our experience of seeing God work to change a challenged community. At the end, I shared the quote that I had shared with our Welfare-to-Work classes on our campus in South Hayward: "If our circumstances are going to change, we must take the brush of faith and paint in vibrant living color on the canvas of our tomorrow."

As I closed my presentation, I asked everyone to stand and place their imaginary easel and canvas in front of them. I then asked participants to close their eyes and see their tomorrow . . . to visualize how it would be different, to capture an image in their minds that would be different from their today. After a few minutes, I asked them to open their eyes, place their paint in the tray in front of them, take their brush in hand, and paint in vibrant living color the picture they had seen. People began to paint. After a few minutes, I asked them to put their brushes down and look at their pictures. To reinforce their mental picture, I asked them to describe it to the person next to them.

At the end, Mr. Covey returned and joined in the applause. He asked me to repeat the quote, and then to my surprise, he asked if he could post the quote on his website. As the class broke for lunch, the shock of the morning continued when Mr. Covey asked, "Bishop, would you join my son and me for lunch."

At lunch, he explained how he had met a Hayward police officer who gave him a detailed story of South Hayward and Pastor Macklin. I was in awe at the amount of information and insight he had. He then requested, "Bishop, would you consider working for us." We both smiled. I'm not sure he was serious. I assured him I was honored, but I had an even higher calling. Within an hour or two, the quote that captured Mr. Covey's attention was on his website, complete with dramatic graphics. There are some experiences you can never forget.

Go ahead now, right where you are, close your eyes and see tomorrow with fresh eyes. See God turning it around . . . see change coming your way. Paint your picture on the canvas of your tomorrow. You can't grasp a vision you can't see. You will never see what could be if you don't know what it must be.

CONSIDER THIS:

1) Describe how Nehemiah's words and actions were both necessary to galvanize the commitment of the people and accomplish their God-sized task?

2) What are some ways you can declare hope in your family, school, career, church, and community? What difference will it make to you?

   . . . to those closest to you?

   . . . to everyone who's watching?

3) What are some specific ways you can partner with your police department, city council, nonprofits, and other organizations to see real change in your city?

4) What events can your church host to declare hope and provide specific resources to people in your area?

5) What is God saying to you in this chapter?

6) Now, at the end of the book, read the last paragraph of this chapter again, and follow the instructions.

WORD ON THE STREET

JOE BRANN

Former Police Chief of Hayward, California
Founding Director of the Office of Community Oriented
Policing Services, U.S. Department of Justice
Founder and CEO of Joseph Brann & Associates, Public Safety Consultants

I spent the bulk of my career with the Santa Ana, California, police department which was one of the first to implement community-oriented policing. In 1989, I was asked to become the police chief in Hayward and tasked with bringing what we'd learned in Santa Ana to the department. Within days of taking the post, the city manager, Lou Garcia, told me, "You really need to meet Pastor Jerry Macklin. He's very interested in working with you in his neighborhood." When we met, I quickly discovered that his vision went far beyond just building his church. He looked for any and every way to add value to the entire neighborhood—not just those who attend his church services.

Jerry is, in my view, a renaissance man. He has been involved in housing, job training, drug rehabilitation, and education, as well as community policing. And he has always found practical, effective ways to meet specific needs. For instance, many of the families in that area of the city were living in severe economically distressed conditions, and the children often didn't have enough to eat. Jerry recruited people from Glad Tidings Church and members of the police department to join together and cook pancake breakfasts on Saturday mornings, with every child in the neighborhood being invited. He ensured there was a safe place and a good meal for them.

Jerry and his church were "force multipliers." They formed working relationships with school administrators, employers, landlords, and agencies to bring resources to those who desperately needed them. One of most powerful parts of his activism was the acquisition of distressed housing and renovating it. One by one, slum dwellings became attractive homes for young families. Drug use declined, gang presence was reduced, household income increased, home values escalated, and the streets became safer. The neighborhood became a place where people actually *wanted* to live. However, none of this just happened. Jerry had a bold vision for the community, and he wasn't willing to take "no" for an answer.

Sometimes people ask, "What was the turning point?" Or "What was the epiphany that changed everything in South Hayward?" It wasn't like that. Jerry has always been relentless in his pursuit of what was best for the people in the neighborhood. There wasn't one moment that changed everything; Jerry orchestrated thousands, maybe tens of thousands, of acts of kindness, evidences of courage, and bold steps to create a vibrant culture in that part of the city. He worked very closely with the members of the city council. He got to know them, he understood their strengths and their passions, and he enlisted them to join him in changing the culture of the community of South Hayward.

He connects exceptionally well with people at all levels—from the powerful to the powerless. He has an uncanny way of finding people who share his heart for the community, or maybe, uncovering and enflaming their hearts to care like he does. Some who are visionaries aren't very good with people, and some who are good with people don't have a compelling vision. Jerry blends vision and compassion better than anyone I've ever known.

Jerry understands that community policing isn't a public relations gimmick. It's about giving people a legitimate stake and a voice in the quality of public safety services, and people served by the police deserve a role in determining how those services should be structured and delivered. We worked together to uncover needs and find solutions, so the community can thrive. He invited everyone—skeptical people on the police force as well as people who had believed the police were prejudiced, uncaring, or corrupt—to the table. Jerry brought understanding and hope to these previously strained relationships, even showing members of the department how much the community was invested in and supported them, and everybody benefitted.

I served as the police chief in Hayward for five years before I went to Washington to become the first Director of the Office of Community Oriented Policing Services, but my friendship with Jerry has never wavered. I still call him to ask for his advice, and he calls me when he needs an understanding ear. If you're Jerry's friend, you're his friend for life.

GLAD TIDINGS
INTERNATIONAL 2.1

The Canvas of 1978 has continued to evolve as the years have progressed. We have never stopped painting, and we are more committed than ever to our leadership mantra: "go as far as you can see, and you will see further." Our current challenge has not been to force the community into the picture we viewed in earlier years; however, to remain committed to the principles and ideals at the root of our ministry as we continue to paint ever more clearly on the canvas of our tomorrow.

Today the city of Hayward has changed in many ways, including in terms of ethnic makeup. Hayward is now the second most diverse city in California. Our Vision for ministry must continue to expand to meet changing demographics and current challenges while seizing opportunities to advance the kingdom agenda.

Through the strength of the Lord, I am so thankful that God has given us grace to take this ministry to Indonesia, Nigeria, South Africa, South America, India, Europe, and points in between.

Through joint efforts with COGIC Charities, Glad Tidings has responded to multiple crises following the Haiti Earthquake and Hurricanes in Texas, Louisiana, and the Bahamas. Today, as blessed as we have been to serve in other places, we continue ministry in our city and throughout Northern California amid the Covid-19 Pandemic. Our South Campus on Tennyson Road serves as a major testing and vaccination site for our South Hayward Community, where tens of thousands have come. In addition to daily food distribution for the past year, on Saturday mornings at our North Campus, an army of GTI volunteers continues to distribute 800 to 1000 boxes of groceries to families in need.

Yes, all of the above gives us reason to be thankful for the strength of the Lord. However, the greater excitement is not the past or the present; the greater excitement is what lies before us on the horizon of Glad Tidings International.

Today, four buildings have come down as we stand ready to erect the new Glad Tidings Life Center on the GTI Campus. This ultra-modern Urban Community Center will allow us to respond to the growing needs of our congregation and community as we expand GTI ministry to the next level. *To God be the Glory for the Canvas of Tomorrow on which we paint.*

APPENDIX

USING *THE CANVAS OF TOMORROW* IN CLASSES AND GROUPS

The Canvas of Tomorrow is designed for individual study, small groups, and classes. The best way to absorb and apply these principles is for each person to individually study and answer the questions at the end of each chapter, and then discuss them in a group environment.

Order enough copies of the book for each person to have a copy.

A recommended schedule for a small group or class might be:

Week 1
Introduce the material. As a group leader, tell your story of learning to trust God for a greater vision of how He might use you. Share your hopes for the group, and provide books for each person. Encourage people to read the assigned chapter each week and answer the questions.

Weeks 2–11
Each week, introduce the topic for the week, and share a story of how God has used the principles in your life. Lead people through a discussion of the questions at the end of the chapter.

Personalize Each Lesson
Don't feel pressured to cover every question in your group discussions. You may have time for all of them, but if not, pick out three or four that had the biggest impact

on you. Focus on those, or ask people in the group to share their responses to the questions that meant the most to them.

Make sure you personalize the principles and applications. At least once in each group meeting, add your own story to illustrate a particular point.

Make the Scriptures come alive. Far too often, we read the Bible like it's a phone book, with little or no emotion. Paint a vivid picture for people. Provide insights about the risk and the power of authentic relationships, and help those in your group sense the emotions of specific people in each scene.

Focus on Application

The questions at the end of each chapter and your encouragement to group members to be authentic will help your group take big steps to apply the principles they're learning. Share how you are applying the principles in particular chapters each week, and encourage them to also take steps of growth.

Three Types of Questions

If you've led groups for a few years, you already understand the importance of using open questions to stimulate discussion. Three types of questions are limiting, leading, and open. Many of the questions at the end of each lesson are open questions.

Limiting questions focus on an obvious answer, such as, "What does Jesus call himself in John 10:11?" They don't stimulate reflection or discussion. If you want to use questions like these, follow them with thought-provoking, open questions.

Leading questions require the listener to guess what the leader has in mind, such as, "Why did Jesus use the metaphor of a shepherd in John 10?" (He was probably alluding to a passage in Ezekiel, but many people don't know that.) The teacher who asks a leading question has a definite answer in mind. Instead of asking this kind of question, you should just teach the point and perhaps ask an open question about the point you have made.

Open questions usually don't have right or wrong answers. They stimulate thinking, and they are far less threatening because the person answering doesn't risk ridicule for being wrong. These questions often begin with "Why do you think . . . ?" "What are some reasons that . . . ?" or "How would you have felt in that situation?"

Preparation

As you prepare to teach this material in a group, consider these steps:

- » Carefully and thoughtfully read the book. Make notes, highlight key sections, quotes, or stories, and complete the reflection section at the end of each chapter. This will familiarize you with the entire scope of the content.
- » As you prepare for each week's group, read the corresponding chapter again and make additional notes.
- » Tailor the amount of content to the time allotted. You may not have time to cover all the questions, so pick the ones that are most pertinent.
- » Add your own stories to personalize the message and add impact.
- » Before and during your preparation, ask God to give you wisdom, clarity, and power. Trust Him to use your group to change people's lives.
- » Most people will get far more out of the group if they read the chapter and complete the reflection each week. Order books before the group or class begins or after the first week.